IF ARISTOTLE RAN GENERAL MOTORS

IF ARISTOTLE RAN GENERAL MOTORS

The New Soul of Business

TOM MORRIS

HENRY HOLT AND COMPANY   NEW YORK

Henry Holt and Company, Inc.
Publishers since 1866
115 West 18th Street
New York, New York 10011

Henry Holt ® is a registered
trademark of Henry Holt and Company, Inc.

Published in Canada by Fitzhenry & Whiteside Ltd.,
195 Allstate Parkway, Markham, Ontario L3R 4T8.

Library of Congress Cataloging-in-Publication Data
Morris, Thomas V.
If Aristotle ran General Motors : the new soul of business / by Tom Morris.—1st. ed.
p.   cm.
ISBN 0-8050-5252-6 (alk. paper)
1. Management—Philosophy.   2. Work—Philosophy.   I. Title.
HD30.19.M67   1997
658—dc21   97-204

Henry Holt books are available for special promotions and
premiums. For details contact: Director, Special Markets.

First Edition 1997

Designed by Kate Nichols

Printed in the United States of America
All first editions are printed on acid-free paper. ∞

1   3   5   7   9   10   8   6   4   2

CONTENTS

PART III: GOODNESS

PART IV: UNITY

Reinventing Corporate Spirit

I f Aristotle ran General Motors, what would he do? How would one of the greatest thinkers and wisest of people in all of human history, the student of Plato and the teacher of Alexander the Great, create lasting excellence and long-term success in the business world of today? What would he focus on? How would he shake things up? If you could magically connect with this great philosopher and seek some personal advice about your business, or about your life, what would he suggest that you pay attention to? What would he advise you to do?

Many of us seem to live stretches of our lives and do our work much of the time as if we think we have to make it all up from scratch as we go along. Or, at best, as if we can only borrow ideas and strategies of action from those people who happen to live and work around us in our own time. We appear to forget that extraordinarily wise people have gone before us, have grappled with many of the same basic issues that we face today, and have bequeathed to us great ideas that we can use.

The philosophers of the centuries, from Plato and Aristotle to the present day, have left us the equivalent of a huge bank account of wisdom that we can draw on for a wealth of insight applicable to both business and the rest of life. We can invest this intellectual capital in our own careers and experiences and reap tremendous returns of new wisdom as a result. If we let the great philosophers guide our thinking, and if we then begin to become philosophers ourselves, we put ourselves in the very best position to move toward genuine excellence, true prosperity, and deeply satisfying success in our businesses, our families, and our lives. Why should we settle for anything less?

> *It may be argued that peoples for whom philosophers legislate are always prosperous.* —ARISTOTLE

In this book I will present some very good news for everyone who cares about the attainment of long-term business excellence and the experience of personal happiness at work amid the turbulent and challenging times we face. This is not a book specifically about General Motors, as distinct from any other contemporary business concerned with basic issues of productivity, competitiveness, and success. I use the name of this famous, paradigmatic American organization in my title as emblematic of any group of people working together. And I won't draw on just the ideas of Aristotle for wisdom, although he will often be my leading light. His name is also to some extent symbolic, representative of all the great thinkers whose insights can shed light on the problems we now face, in business and in life.

But my title also has another deep resonance that I should explain. Testifying before the Senate Armed Services Committee in 1952, the year of my birth, Charles Erwin Wilson, former president of General Motors and later to be Dwight D. Eisenhower's secretary of defense, made one of the most notorious statements of the twentieth century when he proclaimed,

> What is good for the country is good for General Motors, and what's good for General Motors is good for the country.

Critics at the time purported to be stunned by this pronouncement, and commentators ever since have characterized it as a shameless expression of the ultimate in corporate hubris. It seemed to indicate a perverse transvaluation of civic values and betray the radically bloated self-importance not merely of a single company but, more broadly, of industry, commerce, and economics. But when this statement is understood in the most fundamental way possible, I think that it's absolutely right. In this book I will show why.

I believe there are some basic truths, discernible by philosophical reflection, which undergird any sort of human excellence or flourishing, whether in a company like General Motors or in the country at large. In our families, friendships, neighborhoods, communities, civic organizations, and business relationships, four profound but simple foundations—universally accessible, pervasively applicable, and incredibly effective—underlie the attainment and sustaining of the very best results. It is these four foundations, and the path of wisdom they make possible, that we will explore in this book. We'll see that, at bottom, what's good for the country is indeed good for General Motors, and that what's good for General Motors is very good for all the rest of us as well. Regardless of the context, however small or large, whenever people live or work together, the same basic principles must be used to take us to the highest possible level of excellence and keep us there.

I believe that a few simple but powerful ideas drawn from Aristotle as well as from many other great philosophers of the past can help us reenergize our ways of doing business, reinvigorate our workplaces, and reinvent corporate spirit for our time. Ultimately, greatness is rooted in simplicity, if we make consistent use of the most fundamental, simple concepts and truths about excellence as foundations for everything we do.

> *Nothing is more simple than greatness; indeed, to be simple is to be great.* —RALPH WALDO EMERSON

By examining the four simple foundations for all sustainable business and personal excellence, we'll in the end come to see what I think the philosopher Aristotle would focus on if he ran General Motors, if he gave you advice, or even if he helped lead our nation into the future.

Inner Foundations for Excellence

I was recently at a golf resort in Florida with a group of insurance executives. On the first day there, a foursome decided to get in an early round before the formal meetings began. Stepping up to the first tee and making all his normal preparations, the first up of this group took his swing and completely missed the ball. His colleagues, who had played with him many times before, were quite surprised. Without any hesitation, he turned, looked at them with an expression of shock, and said, "Tough course."

The quick-witted golfer revealed with this remark one of the deepest human tendencies. Many of us seem to have an inborn inclination to blame our problems on external circumstances, on forces outside our control. We deflect attention away from ourselves and our own inner states, and focus on something else. Nowhere is this more evident than in modern business. So often we hear about global competition, technological change, the unpredictable economy, organizational restructuring, shareholder demands, or skyrocketing expectations. Tough course.

I suggest that the single most important factor for dealing with all the problems we now face in our business lives is our ability to look within and examine the inner foundations of our own business practices and business relationships. Together we will see how four foundations of human excellence should govern all that we do, both inside our organizations and with all our customers and suppliers.

The key to sustainable success in the world today, I've come to believe, is provided by some of our most ancient wisdom about the human spirit, in the context of our individual lives and our corporate endeavors. Throughout this book we'll focus on the life of business as our springboard for reflection, but we'll find ourselves most often drawing conclusions that apply more broadly to the whole business of life as well.

> *The wisdom of the wise is an uncommon degree of common sense.*
> —DEAN W. R. INGE

I won't be offering in these pages some shockingly new and exotic techniques I've patented for solving all our business and personal problems at the end of the century and into the next millenium. Instead, I'll be using some of the deepest insights of philosophy to articulate and organize a great deal of what you may have long suspected is the proper soil for growing long-lasting human excellence. I'll bring you a template of ideas that will explain quite simply and powerfully why so many business practices that have been found effective do in fact succeed, and why those that don't work fall flat. We're going to step back, philosophically speaking, and take in the big picture of what is needed for truly superior performance and sustainably satisfying outcomes in our time. The foundations for job satisfaction, great corporate spirit, long-term excellence, and lasting success that I'll lay out here will show you new ways to develop what you are already doing right, as well as fundamental ways to correct any problems that may be holding you back.

The Current Climate

For quite a while now American business leaders have been talking about rediscovering the vital importance of product and service quality for financial success in a highly competitive world. In just the past few years, it seems that nearly everyone has been talking about reengineering the corporation, redesigning the processes by which work is done to attain greater efficiencies and new forms of business excellence. Management strategies have multiplied. We're inundated in new techniques and nearly drowning in information. But behind the products, services, and processes of modern business, behind all the strategies and techniques and data, are the people who do the work. And too often, as we have read frequently in the pages of magazines as well as in the panels of comic strips, the employees of modern businesses feel themselves more the victims than the beneficiaries of the new corporate strategies for success. As a result, corporate spirit has suffered immensely.

In fact, it's no exaggeration to say that we live at a time when corporate spirit needs to be reinvented. Pressures from many directions threaten to kill the spirit of productive and creative enterprise, smashing it into shards of cynical mistrust, narrow, destructive self-interest, and increasingly, even low levels of walking despair. Too many people feel insecure, threatened, and unappreciated in their jobs. As a result, their motivation for digging deep and stretching themselves to attain the best of which they're capable has withered. The long-term prognosis for their corporate endeavors cannot be good. In business, as well as in all the professions, and in fact throughout our entire culture, we face a spiritual crisis that is only recently beginning to be recognized as such.

I've come to believe that many companies right now are running on empty and don't realize it, because of the inertia of their organizational processes. If you've drained the tank of human goodwill and motivation, you can continue to coast downhill for a while, even at a pretty rapid clip, but heaven help you if you encounter any big bumps in the road or the competition forces you into an uphill struggle.

> *The greatest asset of any nation is the spirit of its people, and the greatest danger that can menace any nation is the breakdown of that spirit.*
> —GEORGE B. COURTELYOU

People at work are the only true foundation for lasting excellence, and so I think the time has come to focus on the deeply human issues of happiness, satisfaction, meaning, and fulfillment in the workplace. Only by recognizing the vital role of these issues in life and work can we begin the crucial process of reinventing the spirit of our work and sustain excellence into the future. Without this recognition, none of the other strategies for improvement that we pursue—whether reengineering the corporation or refocusing on the needs of the client—will have lasting positive results.

In the large corporation, the small business, the law office, the school, or the medical practice—wherever people work together—we have an urgent need to attend to corporate spirit. As we can see from its Latin root, *corpus*, or "body," the word *corporate* denotes first and foremost any body of people with shared interests or concerns, living together or working together in an organized way. By drawing on ancient wisdom and applying it as a philosopher to what I see happening around me, I've observed that the very same principles that promote human flourishing in personal, family, and friendship contexts apply just as directly to issues of business life and marketplace excellence. But these principles have been almost totally neglected in modern business literature and are insufficiently understood in recent management practice.

People are not motivated to be and do their best unless they feel some significant degree of satisfaction at work. They must sense that their work is a good thing, and doing it must bring them some measure of happiness.

Compensation experts have confirmed again and again that extrinsic rewards like pay raises, promotions, and bonuses can do only so much to motivate extra energy and creativity. This is just as true of negative motivators, like the fear of unemployment, and it holds at every level in the corporation. Without the intrinsic rewards of happiness, fulfillment, and a sense of goodness and meaningfulness at work, people will never be fully motivated to attain and sustain the heights of excellence of which they're capable.

> *The least of things with a meaning is worth more in life than the greatest of things without it.*
> —CARL GUSTAV JUNG

In this book, I will explain how a good dose of ancient wisdom mixed with some contemporary philosophizing about human motivation and human excellence is just what modern business, with its important bottom-line concerns, needs to meet the distinctive challenges that it faces. By using these simple but powerful ideas, we'll be able to put ourselves and our associates into an unparalleled position to move forward productively and establish those conditions that will allow all our corporate activities to flourish.

Bear in mind that reengineering the corporation, and implementing many of the other recently well-publicized fundamental, overall workplace innovations, typically can only be initiated from the top of an organization. By contrast, reinventing corporate spirit can be anybody's job.

Anyone at any level can take the initiative to reinvent corporate spirit within her own field of influence, and can make a difference that may be felt far beyond that domain. Ultimately, what is most important in any organization is also what is most accessible. In the chapters that follow, I'll show how we all together can make a big difference for good by using simple principles that will revolutionize the way we think, not only about our businesses but about our families and communities as well. If Aristotle ran General Motors, I believe that this is what he would get straight first.

ACKNOWLEDGMENTS

I would like to thank all the great people who helped make this book possible: Reid Boates, my literary agent, who brought me together with the wonderful team at Henry Holt and Company; my incredibly insightful editor, Tracy Brown, whose suggestions throughout proved uniformly sagacious; creative hospital president and community philosopher Phil Newbold, who read my very different first draft and had great ideas for changes; my family, who generously gave me the time to write, despite a very busy year; Jamie Wallace, whose daily efforts free me from so many potential distractions; Tom and Mary Parent, whose support means so much; the Advisory Board of the Morris Institute for Human Values; the personal acquaintances whose inspirational stories I tell at various points in the book; and all my new friends in Wilmington and Wrightsville Beach, North Carolina, who help make truth, beauty, goodness, and unity a daily experience. A special word of appreciation to my brother-in-law and his wife, Jerry and Carolyn Teague, who along with Cliff, Melody, and Jeff do so much to make my whole family feel reconnected to our North Carolina roots, and whose many actions on our behalf have made possible so many more rewarding hours of writing than I otherwise could have had. I also thank the numerous companies and professional organizations who have had the audacity to invite a philosopher into their midst, have let me try out these ideas on their turf, and have enthusiastically contributed to their development. I salute you philosophers of business who labor on the front lines daily.

IF ARISTOTLE RAN GENERAL MOTORS

Business Excellence and the Human Quest

The newest problems we face can't be solved without the most ancient wisdom we have. It's time for a wake-up call to summon us all to the enterprise of a little collective philosophy. We've come to a juncture in history when we need to understand the human condition more deeply than ever before and apply that understanding to the way we live and do business every day; the people we live with and do business with will not be satisfied with anything less. Let me tell you a bit about how I have come to this conclusion. First, a little personal background.

Since I grew up in a business family, it was very natural for me to declare a major in business administration when I entered the University of North Carolina at Chapel Hill. Fascinated by business relationships and institutions, I found myself contemplating the study of corporate law, with an eye on preparing for some sort of eventual leadership position in the world of business.

But as I did my coursework, I came to develop an increasing sense of the importance of things I wasn't hearing anyone talk about in my business-related courses. I began to suspect that deeper wisdom about human nature would be important to business in the future, and that if I didn't understand some of the biggest issues that human beings had ever faced, I would never really be able to get my bearings for any of the things I hoped to accomplish.

So I began to study philosophy and religion, examining all the ultimate questions, and every aspect of a big picture for human life and work.

> *Things have their seasons, and even certain kinds of eminence go in and out of style. But wisdom has an advantage: She is eternal.*
> —BALTASAR GRACIÁN

The search for wisdom brought me an undergraduate degree in religion and took me while I was still in college through the writing of my first philosophical book, a small text published a little over a year after my graduation. This same search then sent me to Yale University for graduate school in its renowned department of religious studies. Determined to leave no stone unturned in my quest for ultimate understanding, I ended up becoming only the second person ever to attempt and complete a joint Ph.D. from the two departments of religious studies and philosophy at Yale, a journey of six difficult but often exhilarating years.

While finishing my doctoral dissertation, I also wrote my second book, moved back to North Carolina, had my first child, taught part-time back at the University of North Carolina, and took a North Carolina real estate broker's license on the side, so that I could help my parents with their business should the need arise and keep in touch with the business side of my own interests. A great job in one of the best philosophy departments in the country, however, soon lured me to South Bend, Indiana, where I went on to spend fifteen wonderful years as assistant professor, then associate, then full professor of philosophy at Notre Dame, teaching in some years as much as an eighth of the entire student body and writing nine more academic books of philosophical analysis and reflection for publishers like Oxford, Cornell, and Notre Dame Press. I was in constant interaction with some of the best minds alive all over the world and enjoyed the rare privilege of testing my growing philosophical understanding against the highest standards of intellectual precision.

As I worked with the ideas of the great thinkers of the past, I began to discover powerfully how to be a philosopher in the present. Drawing on their insights, I began to have my own. And this prepared me for an unexpected and remarkable development, a turn of events that would ultimately catapult me over the walls of academia and launch me into an exciting new journey of pioneering exploration as a modern-day philosopher.

The New Wave of Needs and Expectations at Work

A few years ago, I had the most important conversation of my life. I was working hard discharging my professional duties at Notre Dame, striving to master world currents of philosophical reflection, writing up my own discoveries, and lecturing to all the budding sages on campus, when a very active, prominent woman in South Bend heard about my teaching and invited me to give a talk on ethics to a group of young business and civic leaders in town.

I was grateful for the invitation but told her that I had never before given a presentation outside a university context to a nonacademic audience. I was not a business professor or a management consultant. I wasn't sure that what I had to say would hook into the professional interests of the young up-and-comers in local businesses. I was afraid that these junior executives just might not know what to make of a philosopher.

In response to my worry, this young community leader smiled and said something that changed my life.

She replied, "Look, Tom, when I was eighteen and in college, we used to sit up late at night in the dorm and talk about all sorts of important things—life, death, love, meaning, God, happiness, the future, good and evil. Now I'm forty-five years old, and when I get together with friends all that the conversation is ever about is what the kids are doing, what's on sale at the mall, and who Notre Dame is playing this weekend. We never talk about anything important. We've lived long enough to have some real questions and maybe even some answers, but there's never any chance to talk about these big questions with other people. Would you please come into the community and give us an opportunity again to talk and think together about things that really matter? We all need a little philosophy in our lives."

What could I say? She was right. There was a need. And I felt that I should answer the call. But how would people respond? In the ancient world, Socrates had often philosophized in public, giving people the chance to think and talk about important things—with clearly significant consequences, since he ended up being poisoned by popular demand. I hoped for better results, but I never could have imagined what was to happen.

Danger and delight grow on one stalk. —SCOTTISH PROVERB

During the years since that request, I have had an adventure very unusual, and in fact perhaps even unique, for a twentieth-century philosopher. I've flown all over the country, with side trips abroad, to talk to big, enthusiastic groups of real people outside any academic setting about such topics as success, ethics, happiness, personal satisfaction, corporate life, collaborative excellence, and the meaning of it all. I've enjoyed high-energy international wisdom sessions with leaders of the business world. I've visited all sorts of gatherings, from small civic organizations to huge national conventions. I've worked with local companies and multinational corporations. I've spent extensive time with schoolteachers, parents, doctors, lawyers, frontline workers, supervisors, middle managers, and government officials. I've perched on the sofa with Regis and Kathie Lee to pass on some philosophical advice to early-morning America. And I've been stunned by the reaction.

In the midst of all this travel and talk, I've witnessed a very exciting development. In just the last couple of years, everywhere I go across the United States, I've been seeing something I had never anticipated. In the pit of financial difficulties or in the wake of tremendous successes, in places you would never expect it, in good times and bad, people of all sorts are suddenly starting to do something that from my point of view as a philosopher is deeply right.

Having exhausted every other possibility, regular people everywhere suddenly are becoming philosophers. People of all sorts are launching into that engagement of attention and intellect that the woman in my community had so strongly wanted. In every part of the country, I've seen people starting to think in a new way about their work and their lives. They are beginning to philosophize, to reflect deeply on some of their most basic assumptions, and to question how they really want to live. They're tackling the big questions and asking how these issues apply to their lives right now.

> *The true medicine of the mind is philosophy.* —CICERO

Why are so many people beginning to think in this way? Is it to some extent a reaction to the perceived excesses of the eighties? Is this a spiritual backlash to our culture's long-term materialistic fixations? Is it happening in response to the distinctive pressures of the nineties? Could it be that, as we near the close of the most dramatic thousand-year period in human history, it just seems like an appropriate time to take stock, rethink basic priorities and values, and ask questions like "Where are we?" and "Where are we going?"

With the international breakup of the "old world order" and the threat of a new world disorder growing daily, with increasing sensitivity to the pervasiveness of violent crime around the globe, with the ever-increasing pace of change thrown at us by forces seemingly beyond our control, and with our growing awareness of fundamental problems in all our basic social institutions, I think it's safe to say that many people are beginning to feel a bit confused. We all want to get our bearings and make sense of our lives in a time when the meaning of it all is not obvious.

> *To make no mistakes is not in the power of man; but from their errors and mistakes the wise and good learn wisdom for the future.*
> —PLUTARCH

The Vanishing Dream

It wasn't so many years ago that a large percentage of people believed that hard work would always pay off and bring some measure of basic human comfort and security. But we live in a time when those old assurances seem to be quickly disappearing. Men and women can now work their hardest and still find themselves out of a job, for geopolitical or financial reasons that no one seems fully to understand. Increasingly, in job after job, people are being asked to do more and more with less and less, while seeing most of their customary incentives disappear, replaced by that most negative threat of being forced to join the ranks of the unemployed and marginalized. Overall job satisfaction and corporate morale in most places may be at an all-time low. People are disgruntled. They're even despondent. And too many people feel as if they've completely lost their bearings.

So many modern formulas for happiness have failed. Prescriptions for success and promises of a golden age of social well-being have been found empty. There seem to be no easy, ready-made recipes for how to create a deeply satisfying, sustainable way of life, a life truly worth living. This obviously calls for some serious thought. Our time on this earth is not to be wasted.

Philosophy is good advice.   —SENECA

So into the fray steps the age-old pursuit, philosophy. Philosophy is, etymologically, "love of wisdom": the word comes from two ancient Greek roots, *philo,* "love of," and *sophia,* "wisdom." Notice here a small point. It's not *knowledge* of wisdom. It's *love.* Think about this for a moment. If you have an object of love, you embrace it; if you lack it, you pursue it. Philosophy at its best is not just a matter of filling our heads with new questions and deep knowledge. It's also an enterprise of the heart. It is the passionate pursuit and wholehearted embracing of wisdom, or genuine insight about living.

Wisdom is the conqueror of fortune.   —JUVENAL

As I've worked with people in businesses and other organizations all over this country who are currently rethinking their lives, I've formed some strong opinions about exactly what is wrong and what is right in the contemporary business climate. I've come to see what the ancient enterprise of philosophy can contribute toward building sustainable excellence in all our endeavors. And I've also come to understand more deeply than ever before the overall importance of work in our lives, as well as the importance of bringing more of life to work. This has helped me discover a new strategy for workplace transformation that will result powerfully in bringing our work to life.

Business Values
and Personal Commitments

People who are personally reassessing their lives in light of their deepest values will not find it easy to settle for less than a work environment that respects and encourages those values. They will certainly not be able to flourish, to be and do their best, in conditions that have not been wisely developed with sensitivity to what deeply moves people and what most fundamentally matters to us all. The corporate world is unnecessarily losing a great number of very talented people to midlife and midcareer crises. And those who stay are often not contributing all they're capable of. As the big wave of millennial philosophizing begins to crest throughout the population, all of us who aspire to effective leadership and world-class performance had better be ready to surf it. We'd better have our boards in the water, and we'd better be paddling in the right direction, because this one's going to be a tsunami, and it will take us further than anything else possibly could.

> The mark of wisdom is to read aright the present, and to march with the occasion. —HOMER

And so that's what this book is about: catching the new wave of wisdom at work today and creating the right environment for ultimate motivation in the workplace. Laying the right foundations for long-term business excellence is a matter of bringing the deepest, most naturally renewable motivation into all our endeavors together. Many companies bring in motivational speakers on a regular basis to inspire the troops for an hour, or a day, or a week. But these seeds of inspiration must be dropped into fertile soil if they're to take root and produce results. And so we're going to see what the great thinkers might have to say about enriching the soil, enhancing the environment, laying down new conditions for superior work, and reaping the consequences in a surprisingly short period of time.

> He is not wise to me who is wise in words only, but he who is wise in deeds. —SAINT GREGORY

As the first-century Stoic thinker Seneca once said, "The best ideas are everyone's property." If we take possession of them and use them well, we'll see a tremendous difference for all our enterprises.

Aristotle and the Human Quest

The great philosopher Aristotle saw deeply into human nature. And that's no surprise. For twenty years he was a close student of and companion to Plato, one of the most creative and expansive of minds in all of human history, and Plato himself had learned to think critically and imaginatively from the master Socrates, whom the Roman orator, philosopher, and statesman Cicero later described as the first man ever to bring philosophy into the marketplace.

> *Some wisdom must be learned from one who is wise.*   —EURIPIDES

Socrates, who lived from about 470 to 399 B.C., gave us the first model of a man engaged in courageous questioning in search of true wisdom. His student Plato, sojourning on this earth from the years of 428 to 348 B.C., had such an extensive impact on Western thought with his writings that Harvard philosopher and mathematician Alfred North Whitehead would in our century describe the whole history of philosophy as just a series of footnotes to Plato. And yet Aristotle, who lived from 384 to 322 B.C. and was the beneficiary of both Socrates and Plato, combined the pragmatic ethical interests of Socrates with the systematic mentality of Plato. He brought a talent for careful observation into the service of an incredible analytical ability to see beneath the surface of life. And whenever he thought about human nature, he had insights that are to this day unrivaled for profundity and power. So it's to a pivotal piece of his wisdom that we now turn to get our bearings.

When he looked around at the world, Aristotle saw, as all of us do, that human beings pursue different things. Some seek wealth. Others dream of fame. Some long for love. Others lust for power. The cautious aim for security, the bold look for adventure. But Aristotle had the insight that beneath all the surface differences in what we seem to chase, everyone in this life is really after the same thing: happiness. And what Aristotle discerned, many subsequent thinkers have confirmed.

> *All men seek happiness. This is without exception. Whatever different means they employ, they all tend to this end. The cause of some going to war, and of others avoiding it, is the same desire in both, attended with different views. The will never takes the least step but to this object. This is the motive of every action of every man, even of those who hang themselves.*   —BLAISE PASCAL

The president of the company, the shipping clerk, the office manager, the salesman, the accountant, the current client, the potential customer, the supplier, and every other person you come in contact with during the day is seeking, in everything they do, to be happy. This is the universal human quest, underlying every other activity. If we can come to understand most deeply what that happiness is which we all seek, we can touch the innermost heart of human motivation and unlock the deepest secret of sustainable success in all our efforts together. Simple, but powerful.

What, then, is happiness? What is it exactly that we all pursue? If we can understand this, we can come to see more deeply what it is that people need to experience in their work as well as in their personal lives. Surprisingly, from all the great thinkers reflecting on the topic of happiness throughout the centuries and across all the major world cultures, I believe that we have inherited only three basic views of happiness. One of them will give us the keys that we need for unlocking individual potential and creating the innermost foundations for long-term business excellence.

The first understanding of happiness comes to us from the distant past, but it is this view that has dominated the perspectives of so many people in the twentieth century. To give it expression, let me quote a man who, for many years before his death, was one of my favorite ancient thinkers, comedian George Burns. He once said, mirroring a famous eighteenth-century French philosopher but with his own distinctive twist, "Happiness is—a good meal, a good cigar, and a good woman. Or a bad woman, depending on how much happiness you can stand."

> *Happiness: a good bank account, a good cook, and a good digestion.*
> —JEAN-JACQUES ROUSSEAU

In his inimitable way, this classic American scalawag was attempting to articulate the hedonistic view of the ages: Happiness is just the same thing as pleasure. The advice of those who take this view is, if you want happiness, pursue pleasure and seek to avoid pain.

Happiness as Pleasure

It's this view of happiness that's behind the nearly frantic modern quest for money and things. Novelist Jane Austen is often quoted as having said over a hundred years ago, "A large income is the best recipe for happiness I ever heard of." Of course, it seems that people chase money and hope for a large income primarily to get other things, the things they think will make them happy, or at least contribute significantly to their happiness. Concerning those most general things that people notoriously seek in their pursuit of happiness—money, fame, power, and status—the hedonistic view would be that they are sought because they bring pleasure either in themselves or in what they make possible, and that it is precisely the pleasure they provide that is the essence of happiness.

> *Money's easy to make if it's money you want. But with few exceptions people don't want money. They want luxury and they want love and they want admiration.* —JOHN STEINBECK

But is happiness the same thing as pleasure?

Aristotle once characterized this belief as a view fit for grazing cattle but not human beings. In our own century, Albert Einstein echoed Aristotle; commenting on any worldview that puts happiness, viewed as pleasure, at the center, he wrote, "In this sense I have never looked upon ease and happiness as ends in themselves—such an ethical basis I call more proper for a herd of swine." Strong words, but for a good point.

For all its importance in human life, pleasure is just one piece of a much larger puzzle. I can't imagine a happy life utterly devoid of enjoyment, but pleasure is not the same thing as happiness. The occasional self-destructive behavior of the rich and famous confirms this far too vividly.

> *Many who seem to be struggling with adversity are happy; many, amid great affluence, are utterly miserable.* —PUBLIUS CORNELIUS TACITUS

Happiness is not identical to pleasure. And that's a good thing if we seek happiness at work, because the workday is not usually just one long wave of pleasure washing over us. Nonetheless, there should be as many pleasures as possible connected with our work. People do their best when they enjoy what they are doing. And extrinsic rewards can indeed help provide for an enhanced ongoing enjoyment of the work experience. People should be well paid for what they do, and it's important to give associates the recognition they deserve for a job well done. Status can also be properly aspired to and attained in even a flattened organization. Promotion up a managerial hierarchy is not a necessary condition for the accruing of positive status. We can honor people in many ways, and increased power can and should be awarded to our colleagues who demonstrate their ability to use power well.

Certainly, the enjoyment of money, status, recognition, and power can be properly recognized as contributing to a happy life, or at least a happy workplace experience, if these things are received and used well. But the need for that little qualification alone, that little "if," is enough to indicate that the potential pleasures of money, fame, power, and status are not themselves the same thing as happiness. As we'll see shortly, what matters most is the overall process in which these enjoyments have a place. If we want the people around us to experience a measure of happiness in the business we do together, and if we ourselves want to be happy in our work, we have to cast our net beyond the considerations of compensation, recognition, regard, and power alone. But then we are still left asking what exactly happiness is.

Let's examine a second view of happiness that comes to us from antiquity, one associated with Stoic philosophy in the West, and with many strands of philosophical thinking in the East. For reasons we'll discuss, this view has held great attraction for people in the late twentieth century, especially for those who see the limits of pleasure in human life. It is the view that happiness is ultimately personal peace.

> *A happy life consists in tranquillity of mind.* —CICERO

Happiness as Personal Peace

Tranquillity. Equanimity. Calm. Imagine the spirit of a happy person as mirrored by the surface of a still pond on a windless day. This is the goal of the meditative techniques practiced by people in every walk of life. I recently met a late-middle-aged conservative gentleman who couldn't get over what was going on in his own family. In describing what was to him a surprising development in the life of a family member, he shrugged and said, a bit sheepishly, "My son's taken up meditation. I guess it beats sittin' doin' nothin'." Well of course it *is* sitting doing nothing, but in the best possible way, with the purpose of obtaining ultimate inner peace.

Clearly we could all use a little more calm in our lives. The *Los Angeles Times Magazine* not long ago did a cover story called "The New Age of Anxiety: At the End of the American Century, the Country Is Stressed Out." Anxiety in America has reached epidemic proportions. People are worried about their jobs, their marriages, their neighborhoods, their kids, their future. And it doesn't only start when one has a family to support and a mortgage to pay. Elementary-school-age kids now regularly talk about being "stressed out," and teachers increasingly share with preteens physical and mental strategies for handling the pressures of modern life.

This is every bit as serious as it is pervasive. On an airplane recently I read a newspaper article about anxiety being a significant health risk; a recent study on thousands of adults had indicated that highly nervous individuals are four times likelier than the rest of the population to be victims of sudden heart death. I thought to myself, "Reading *this* is not going to help the nervous people a whole lot." But it's true. Anxiety kills. It kills the spirit and the body. And we need to overcome it.

The ancient Stoic philosophers believed that nothing in the world is either as good or as bad as it seems. They realized that many people are nervous wrecks because they become too excited about the good things and too depressed about the bad. We need something like inner psychic shock absorbers as we hit the potholes and speed bumps of life, a measure of inner peace that will allow us to be flexible and steady amid all those unexpected things that life throws at us. We all need to calm down.

> *There is no joy but calm.* —ALFRED, LORD TENNYSON

But the very pace of modern life militates against calmness. In the 1950s, social scientists predicted that by the end of the century we'd all be living lives of leisure. Technology would free us from dull, time-consuming tasks and allow us to work four-hour days, twenty-hour weeks, maybe less. Why do you think that so many of our colleges and universities during this period began setting up departments of recreation administration and leisure studies? It wasn't because they needed special classes for their football teams. It was to help us figure out what to do with all the predicted spare time we would be experiencing.

Of course, that prophesied age of leisure has not materialized. On the contrary, life has gone into fast-forward. Cell phones, pagers, microwaves, instant grits. . . . I recently caught myself hovering over my fax machine in a state of high anxiety, gesturing wildly at the paper coming out of the slot, and saying *out loud* in a voice of frustration, "Faster! Faster!"

It's gone too far. A reporter and essayist named Joel Achenbach has written about a current research project to design portable cellular phones as cochlear implants. The receiver would be medically implanted in your ear, and the transmitter would be a cap on your tooth. Can you imagine this? "Doctor, doctor, there's a ringing in my ears!" "Well, answer it, you fool!"

What is the point of all this silliness? The external world will never move us toward nirvana. It might, on the contrary, drive us crazy. And we can't live happily with our nerves all ajangle. We need some calm. We need inner peace. We need some measure of personal tranquillity or we'll never be able to deal well with all that the future may throw at us.

The Stoic philosophers were right in believing that peacefulness is important. A happy life utterly devoid of personal peace is impossible. But is peace the same thing as happiness? As a wonderful and wise author named Mary Ann Evans, who wrote over one hundred years ago under the pen name George Eliot, once put it, "It is vain to say that human beings ought to be satisfied with tranquillity: they must have action; and they will make it if they cannot find it."

> *A life at ease is a difficult pursuit.* —WILLIAM COWPER

In his great book, *Man's Search for Meaning*, Victor Frankl put it like this:

I consider it a dangerous misconception of mental hygiene to assume that what man needs in the first place is equilibrium or, as it is called in biology, "homeostasis," i.e., a tensionless state. What man actually needs is not a tensionless state but rather the struggling and striving for a worthwhile goal, a freely chosen task. What he needs is not the discharge of tension at any cost but the call of a potential meaning waiting to be fulfilled by him.

> *Happiness is not a station that you arrive at, but a manner of travelling.* —MARGARET LEE RUNBECK

Too many people in the business world today seem to resent the challenges coming their way and hanker after equilibrium, a tranquillity in the work environment that would in effect render them, as human problem solvers, quite superfluous. But we humans don't grow amid utter tranquillity. We need action. We need problems. We need a healthy amount of tension in our lives. Human happiness is not to be thought of as the emotional equivalent of one long nap. To help the people around us be happy at work, we may indeed need to help them calm their nerves a bit on occasion, but happiness at work does not require total workplace serenity. There is complete quietude only in death, and business is an activity of the living.

> *But men must know, that in the theater of man's life it is reserved only for God and the angels to be lookers on.* —FRANCIS BACON

In their own ways, George Eliot and Victor Frankl were making a point articulated centuries before by Aristotle, when he concluded, "Happiness is a sort of action." Let me dress it out a little bit and offer this definition in the spirit of Aristotle: Happiness is participation in something that brings fulfillment.

Happiness as Participation in Something Fulfilling

In his essay *De Finibus*, the Roman statesman and practical philosopher Cicero proclaimed, "The soul ever yearns to be doing something." It is not having but doing that is most intimately related to the fullest experience of being. We are at our best and feel our best when we are engaged in a worthy task.

> *I arise in the morning torn between a desire to improve (or save) the world and a desire to enjoy (or savor) the world. This makes it hard to plan the day.*
> —E. B. WHITE

Recently, when I was giving a number of talks over a short period of time in Disney World, my wife bought me the authorized biography of Walt Disney to give me some perspective on his legacy. Let me quote a snippet from one of his conversations that will be particularly illuminating here:

> I've always been bored with just making money. I've wanted to do things, I wanted to build things. Get something going . . . I'm not like some people who worship money as something you've got to have piled up in a big pile somewhere. I've only thought of money in one way, and that is to do something with it. . . . I don't think there is a thing that I own that I will ever get the benefit of, except through doing things with it.

I believe that Walt Disney was an Aristotelian about happiness. It was never a matter of just piling up money or stuff to be enjoyed. It was always a matter of the joy of doing, of creating, of participating in the building of new things to enrich the world.

> *It is only well with me when I have a chisel in my hand.*
> —MICHELANGELO

Happiness is not the same thing as pleasure, and it's not the same as personal peace. Both of these are relatively passive states, however active we may sometimes be in our pursuit of them. Happiness never exists in passivity. It is in fact a dynamic phenomenon of participation in something that brings fulfillment. At its best, it is accompanied by pleasure and a good measure of inner peace. In fact, it can be argued that one of the highest forms of peace is that which accompanies satisfying engagement in a job worth doing. And one of the greatest pleasures in life is active fulfillment from a job well done. So happiness is connected with peace as well as with pleasure. But ultimately it is to be found in the activity. It is in the work.

> *Taste the joy that springs from labor.*
>
> —HENRY WADSWORTH LONGFELLOW

But this new definition of happiness immediately raises an obvious question. What exactly does bring fulfillment to human beings? It's one thing to be told that happiness is participation in something that brings fulfillment, but we won't understand what that means, or exactly what happiness is, and what this implies for organizational or business motivation, until we get clear what it is that brings us fulfillment. Let's consider two answers.

The first is simple: different things for different people. Maybe you experience a sense of fulfillment working with a lot of other people in a large, open office. Maybe someone else is fulfilled in a more solitary routine. Perhaps you derive a measure of fulfillment in your personal time from playing music. Maybe I like sports. Different things for different people.

This answer is true, but it's also superficial. The greatest thinkers have seen that there is a fundamental unity beneath the apparent diversity of forms of human fulfillment. My second answer to the question of what brings fulfillment to people takes this into account. I've come to believe that an activity or enterprise, a relationship or involvement, a form of work or a form of play, can contribute to bringing fulfillment to the people involved in it only if it respects and nurtures four fundamental dimensions of human experience.

We're going to explore in detail what these four dimensions are, but I should say right off that they are four basic ways that we all experience the world around us as we live every day. All our senses can be involved in each of these modes of apprehending life. And everything we do can reflect these four dimensions. This structure of our experience is universal, because it is rooted in human nature at the most basic level.

> *Nature has given the opportunity of happiness to all, knew they but how to use it.*
>
> —CLAUDIAN

This is the ultimate existential unity beneath the manifest diversity of human life. Whether you're single or married, employed or unemployed, a doctor, lawyer, factory line supervisor, or company president, a mother or an elected official, whether you're in sales and service or research and development, whatever your place in this world, you will not be fulfilled in whatever it is that you're doing unless these four basic dimensions of your experience are addressed. And the people around you won't experience a measure of fulfillment or happiness in that relationship or activity with you either unless these same dimensions of their experience are being nurtured as well.

The ancient philosophers wrote a lot about these dimensions, along with the foundations they provide for human fulfillment, and they were appreciated by medieval thinkers as well. Saint Thomas Aquinas (1225–1274), for instance, had his way of explicating what have come to be known to us as the great transcendentals, and William of Occam (c. 1285–1349) had his own distinct way too. What I will present to you here owes a lot to the work of other thinkers, but it is primarily the product of my own thought and experience and so comes to you with no other imprimatur but the testimony I offer and the confirmation you see in your life and career. I am convinced that this powerful framework captures the best of what has been thought on the subject and in fact delineates the lineaments of ultimate reality as they impinge universally on issues of human happiness and workplace excellence. But in the end it is up to each of us to put these ideas to the test and prove them in our own experience.

Let me indicate briefly what these four crucial dimensions of human experience are. They will structure all the rest of what I have to say in this book. They are that important.

The Four Dimensions of Human Experience

There are four basic dimensions to all human experience, across all world cultures and throughout all of our history. They are as important now as they have ever been. They're the keys to individual happiness at work as well as sustainable corporate excellence. And yet they are only recently coming to be understood and appreciated for their true significance in modern business. Each of the dimensions leads to a goal, a target that is itself a bedrock foundation for enduring human fulfillment. They are:

1. The Intellectual Dimension, which aims at Truth

2. The Aesthetic Dimension, which aims at Beauty

3. The Moral Dimension, which aims at Goodness

4. The Spiritual Dimension, which aims at Unity

The Intellectual, the Aesthetic, the Moral, and the Spiritual: Truth, Beauty, Goodness, and Unity. These are the elements that structure all of human life. And they offer us four timeless virtues, or strengths, for the soul of any productive endeavor with other people, and thus four foundations for sustainable human excellence. We neglect them in our business lives to our great peril.

Let me put it again in a simple chart:

THE FOUR DIMENSIONS OF HUMAN EXPERIENCE	THE FOUR FOUNDATIONS OF HUMAN EXCELLENCE
The Intellectual	Truth
The Aesthetic	Beauty
The Moral	Goodness
The Spiritual	Unity

I've become convinced that these four dimensions of experience, and these four foundations of excellence, provide us with the key to both rediscovering personal satisfaction at work and reinventing corporate spirit in our time. They are the key to sustainable corporate excellence because they are the foundations of corporate fulfillment, and they have that status because they are the deepest touchstones for ultimate individual fulfillment and happiness.

People will not have a sense of positive corporate spirit in any endeavor unless that activity is connected with their personal quest for happiness, unless they are feeling some degree of fulfillment and some measure of happiness in that task. And it is only when this issue of individual fulfillment is understood in the deepest possible way that we will see how personal satisfaction is finally tied to interpersonal, organizational, and business flourishing.

As we look at the applications of truth, beauty, goodness, and unity in personal and corporate life, we're going to be examining the inner foundations for sustainable excellence in all our business endeavors. It is the people within any enterprise, and their interactions with each other, that ultimately produce excellence or mediocrity.

One of the most creative scientists alive, MacArthur Award winner Dr. John Holland of the University of Michigan, has said of any sufficiently complex system, "We can't add up the parts and understand the whole, for that does not give a good picture of what the system does. The interactions are just as important as the parts." In this same way what we're going to be exploring together here is the way in which the most fundamental parts of any business system, any organization or business relationship—the people who make it go—must operate and interact for that system to attain long-term excellence. Only by grasping this will we really understand business excellence and business success in the deepest possible way.

I
TRUTH

1

The Intellectual Dimension at Work

The first universal dimension of human experience is the intellectual dimension, that aspect of our nature which aims at truth.

Every human being has a mind. Each of us has an intellectual dimension to his experience. We need ideas as much as we need food, air, or water. Ideas nourish the mind as the latter provide for the body. In light of this, it's clear that we need good ideas as much as we need good food, good air, and good water. And, finally, what we need is truth.

> *The soul is unwillingly deprived of truth.* —EPICTETUS

Truth is just that mapping of reality that corresponds to the way things are. Put another way, it is the relationship of accuracy that holds between a good map and the territory it represents. Aristotle wrote about truth, in contrast to falsehood, in this way: "To say of what is that it is not, or of what is not that it is so, is false; while to say of what is so that it is so, and of what is not so that it is not so, is true." Perhaps this is enough to make you glad that you're reading me rather than Aristotle. Truth is our lifeline. Truth is our guide. The truth about truth is simple.

No one can navigate well through life without an accurate map by which to steer. Knowledge is the possession of such a map, and truth is what that map gives us, linking us to reality. The absolutely vital importance of knowledge in any business is beginning to be widely recognized. For discerning the needs of clients, monitoring the moves of competitors, benefiting from the experience of associates, and serving others well, it's hard to see how there could be anything ultimately more important than truth.

But it may be that the simple importance of truth is still far from widely enough appreciated. It's often been said that people nowadays must view truth as precious, they use it so sparingly. Even this little witticism contains some insight.

> As hypocrisy is said to be the highest compliment to virtue, the art of lying is the strongest acknowledgment of the force of truth.
>
> —WILLIAM HAZLITT

People who tell the truth, however difficult that may be, obviously have a high regard for its importance. But even people who lie to you indicate in a backward sort of way their partial, and deeply flawed, recognition of at least some of the power of truth: They think of it as too powerful to be entrusted to you.

Is truth both important and powerful in our corporate endeavors? And, if so, then how should we treat the truth? How, correspondingly, should we treat each other with regard to the truth? These are some of the questions we'll address both in this chapter and in the next one.

> Those who know the truth are not equal to those who love it, and they who love it are not equal to those who delight in it.
>
> —CONFUCIUS

Truth and Respect

We all have minds that must be respected and used. The first implication of this is that mindless work cannot be satisfying. No human being is a machine, and yet that's exactly what much of the economic theory and management practice of the last hundred years has tended to assume.

Don Petersen, past president of Ford Motor Company, tells an interesting story. Once when he was visiting a stamping plant in Buffalo, New York, a huge bear of a man came up to him and said, "You know, I want to tell you one thing. I used to hate coming to work here. But lately I've been asked what I think, and that makes me feel like I'm somebody. I never thought the company saw me as a human being. Now I like coming to work."

One of the most ennobling gestures any of us can make toward another human being is to ask her, sincerely, what she thinks about what we are doing together. What is her take on the truth? When we ask, wanting to hear, we treat the other person with a fundamental respect, and this behavior is then much more likely to be mirrored back to us.

We should cultivate an environment in which people are not afraid to tell us the truth. We need the truth if we are to steer safely through the difficulties we may face as we move into the future, and we're unlikely to get enough of it unless others are open to sharing it with us. Too many frontline workers and managers are reluctant to pass on a hard truth to the person they report to, because they are working in a corporate culture where it's not clear what the value of truth is.

> *I search after truth, by which man never yet was harmed.*
>
> —MARCUS AURELIUS

In a recent book in which he profiled three of the top corporate CEOs recognized as masters at company renovation—Jack Welch (General Electric), the late Mike Walsh (Union Pacific Railroad), and Percy Barnevik (Asea Brown Boveri), Tom Peters points to eleven traits that seem responsible for their success. One of these eleven qualities, he says, is that these individuals appear to have "a visceral affinity for truth." The capacity to handle the truth, the ability to get at it, and the skill to use it well brings with its exercise great power. We aren't likely to be expert at exercising that capacity unless we place a certain value on the people around us. And this is an important issue in renewing corporate spirit.

A few years ago I met Tom Chappell, founder of Tom's of Maine, a highly regarded personal care products company. In the course of a morning together sitting and talking on the front porch of a beautiful house in Vermont, I heard one of the most interesting leadership stories in contemporary American business.

Tom had established his company on strong moral principles, but as the business grew and more people were hired for their technical expertise in managing that growth, Tom began to feel that the company was drifting away from its founding vision. To regain his grip on those values that ought to govern business lives, he decided to take a sabbatical of sorts and go for part of each week to the Harvard Divinity School, where he enrolled as a student. Now, notice clearly, we're talking about the Harvard *Divinity* School, not the Harvard *Business* School. The company's board thought Tom had lost his mind. They didn't understand that he was just trying to find his soul.

One of the most important discoveries he made in his studies was the writings of Martin Buber, an influential Jewish theologian who lived from 1878 until 1965. In his book *I and Thou*, Buber explains that there are basically two fundamental relationships that can exist between you and another individual entity in this world. First, there is the I–It relation. This is a way of relating to something as a thing, or object, whose only value is extrinsic, or instrumental. When you stand in the I–It relation to something, you value it only insofar as it serves your purposes. This is the relationship you have toward a cup whose only value consists in its ability to hold the water you're drinking and to convey that drink in an efficient way into your mouth. This is the relationship you have with a copy machine whose only value is to duplicate documents, or to a computer that is no more than what it does, or rather, allows you to do.

The second basic relationship, Buber calls the I–Thou relation. This is the fundamental stance that one human being ought always to take toward another person, a relationship of respect in which the other individual is viewed as having intrinsic value, value in and of himself or herself, regardless of whether that individual can produce any further value for you.

> *If you have some respect for people as they are, you can be more effective in helping them to become better than they are.*
>
> —JOHN GARDNER

In the tradition of the great German philosopher Immanuel Kant (1724–1804), Buber holds that one human being should never treat another person only as a means to some extrinsic end but primarily and always as an end in himself. We should never use other people precisely in the way that we use objects. This of course doesn't mean that you can't ask another person to bring you a document, make a phone call, or run some numbers for you on a new account. What it means is that you should never view other people as having value only for what they can do for you.

The I–Thou stance is one of respect and dignity. That's why we are using the somewhat archaic word "Thou." It's commonly used in English to translate one of two German pronouns for what's called grammatically the second person. The English "you" is used to translate the more familiar of the two terms, which connotes a casual sort of friendliness, whereas the other German term, which conveys a more formal dignity or respect, is rendered by "Thou."

When Tom Chappell came to understand this distinction, he realized that his company had drifted into an I–It relationship with its customers, viewing them as if their only value was the money they could provide. And if that's how we view our customers, he concluded, why should they want to give us their money? Tom used the work of Buber, as well as that of other philosophers and theologians, to turn things around and change people's attitudes within the company so that they could become the exemplary organization they are now known to be. The whole story is told in an exciting and masterful way in Tom's recent book *The Soul of a Business*.

> *Veracity is the heart of morality.* —T. H. HUXLEY

For our purposes at present, the powerful point is this. When we do not create an environment in which truth is respected, we do not have a working environment in which people are being respected. The only way to enter a truly I–Thou relationship with those around us is to seek from them, and give to them, the truth about what we are doing together. This is the only way to treat coworkers. And this is the way to treat both suppliers and vendors on one side, and all our customers or potential customers on the other.

To the extent that you are truthful with another person, you show that individual respect. When you sincerely ask the other person what she thinks, you show respect as well. Any time you genuinely seek a customer's input, and really listen, you treat that customer as a Thou. This is at the heart of a morally sound relationship. And, done in the right spirit, it is always appreciated. Given and received properly, a concern with sharing truth inevitably helps to generate a spirit of cooperation crucial to good working relations over the long run.

Knowledge and the Need for Truth

Truth is the foundation for trust, and nothing is more important for any business endeavor than trust. Trust is an absolute necessity for truly effective interpersonal activity.

> *If people who have to work together in an enterprise trust one another because they are all operating according to a common set of ethical norms, doing business costs less.* —FRANCIS FUKUYAMA

It's said often that we are moving quickly into an information economy. We need to think about the relevance of this to how we treat each other in the course of doing our work. Do we provide the people who work around us with all the information they might benefit from having? Or do we withhold information until we perceive an absolute need for its dissemination?

We are rightly concerned these days about greater efficiency in our businesses. We've increasingly come to understand how important this is to sustainable competitiveness. We need to ferret out and eliminate sources of waste and inefficiency wherever they exist. But here we come to something almost never discussed when efficiency is analyzed. There is probably no greater source of wasted time and energy in modern corporate life than the distraction that arises when truth is not readily available in the workplace and speculation, gossip, and rumor rush in to fill the void.

Without all the facts relevant to their jobs, people feel lost and sense a lack of control over their lives and destinies. Nature does abhor this kind of vacuum. Human beings can't stand to feel helpless, so to compensate, they latch on to the first notion around that looks like relevant fact. And then the speculation or gossip spreads like fire, consuming the hearts and minds of the people it touches.

> *Nothing is swifter than rumor.* —VIRGIL

Human beings can't do without truth. If they don't have the genuine article, they'll fall for anything that passes for it. And this can create serious problems for any company.

As the Spanish-born Roman poet Martial wrote in the first century, "Conceal a flaw and the world will imagine the worst." Whenever you confront a problem, you confront the need for truth. The people who work with you can't be their best if they are busy imagining the worst concerning the state of the company, what you think of their performance, or what the future might hold. Truth, even hard truth, if passed on with as much understanding, kindness, and sensitivity as possible, is always the foundation for solving any problem in a sustainable way.

> *Such is the irresistible nature of truth that all it asks, and all it wants, is the liberty of appearing.* —THOMAS PAINE

A neighbor of mine worked at General Electric for many years, reporting directly to Jack Welch. It was his job to go in to GE businesses that were underperforming and either turn them around or shut them down. He tells me that the most effective policy was to announce to everyone right away why he was there, what the whole situation was, and what needed to be done if they were to survive as a business. Making available the truth, however difficult, always bolstered morale and gave the people involved their best shot at success. When his counterparts in other companies avoided doing this, he inevitably saw a mess of speculation, gossip, and despair, with sinking morale, decreasing productivity, and inevitable failure as the result.

In his book *The Corporate Coach*, James B. Miller tells the story of his remarkable company Miller Business Systems and Business Interiors, often cited as having one of the highest customer-retention rates among similar companies in the country. Early on in the book, he advises what to do when a problem will affect a customer. He says, "Go to the customer with the truth." Simple. And effective. He goes on to warn against any other strategy and says straight out, *"Nothing but the truth will do"* (his emphasis).

Soon after writing these words, I had a small personal experience that illustrates this point. I took my family out for lunch at one of their favorite restaurants. After placing our order, we seemed to have an unusually long time to chat and admire the decor. Usually prompt service complements the good food in this establishment, and as the minutes dragged on I began to wonder whether the young man who took our order had been a mischievous college kid pulling a prank with his best waiter impersonation. And we sat. Finally, as he dashed by, I asked this gentleman in the nicest of ways when I might expect to receive my soup. He looked astonished, as if we were speaking for the first time, said "Just a minute," and disappeared again. Was he going to talk to a fraternity brother in the back of the restaurant pretending to be a chef? In a moment the manager appeared, apologizing that our order had somehow been lost in the kitchen, and telling us that the meal would be on the house.

That one act of telling us the truth and taking responsibility for the consequences transformed us from casual sometime visitors into very loyal customers. The manager didn't have to come out. I had not made a fuss. Even if I had complained and asked to see him, he could have tried to excuse the delay with a flustered allegation of busyness and brushed us off. He didn't. He told the truth. And, of course, it isn't irrelevant that he also paid for the meal. But even without that additional kind gesture, the Rockola Café would have won us over in a new way. The manager went beyond the call of duty to repair a possibly damaged relationship, told the truth, and thereby brought it about that the relationship would grow to a new level.

In business, as in every other facet of life, relationships rule the world. A relationship built on falsehood is like a house built on sand; one built on truth is like a fortress anchored in rock. In his important recent book *Relationship Marketing,* Regis McKenna has pointed out that the corporate fads of the eighties are finally being superseded by a new wisdom. He believes that, instead of continuing to see companies lurching from one purported quick fix to another to improve their business position, we'll now begin to witness something very different. Henceforth, he says, "Companies will seek to achieve a superior position by building solid relationships with their customers: relationships based on trust, responsiveness, and quality." As we've seen, it's the first item in this list, trust, which is impossible over the long term without the deeper foundation of truth.

> *Truth is man's proper good, and the only immortal thing was given to our mortality to use.* —BEN JONSON

Whenever you tell another person the truth, you show, to that extent, some measure of respect for that person, respect he will typically appreciate and most likely reciprocate. I say that you show respect "to that extent" because it is of course possible to speak truthfully yet insultingly. A fascinating aspect of our four-dimensional framework for human fulfillment and the corresponding four foundations for excellence is that each of these dimensions must be respected and nurtured, and each of these foundations implemented, in the governing context of the other three for genuine happiness and real human flourishing to result.

Accordingly, the truth must always be handled in such a way as to be consistent with beauty, goodness, and unity for its use to convey proper respect to another person. The deep interconnections between the four foundations of truth, beauty, goodness, and unity will be significant at every juncture. Correspondingly, the connectedness of the four dimensions of human experience is just as important as the inner essence of any one of them.

> *Thanks to words, we have been able to rise above the brutes; and thanks to words, we have often sunk to the level of demons.*
>
> —ALDOUS HUXLEY

Without an understanding of this point, truth-telling can have a corrosive impact on a relationship or on an office. We've all been around people who seem to delight in voicing awkward truths at inappropriate times with the apparent intent to hurt others. This is not living productively in the truth, but rather using the truth as a weapon.

The Double Power Principle

There is a universal principle that seems to govern all of life, which I like to call the double power principle. It is as simple as it is profound:

To the extent that something has power for good, it has corresponding power for ill. Most of the time, it's up to us how we use that power.

Consider common examples of this. Nuclear energy has tremendous power for good, as illustrated by nuclear medicine. But it even more obviously has horrific power for ill, as captured in nuclear weaponry. And think for a moment about the phenomenon of human desire. Without the existence of desire among human beings, we would never have created or built anything. Culture and civilization would not exist. But desire out of control is responsible for a great many of the social, political, and personal problems of the world.

> *The greater the power, the more dangerous the abuse.*
> —EDMUND BURKE

In a speech on success and ethics to a large business group, I happened to mention the spiritual aspect of human life a couple of times. Afterward, while telling me how deeply he appreciated the substance of my talk, the president of the company added, "But let me ask you about one thing. I noticed you mentioned spirituality near the end of the talk. The point you made struck me as important, even though I've always been very cautious about organized religion. So many terrible things have been done in the name of religion over the centuries."

Even though I had not mentioned organized religion in my talk, it was natural to make the connection. This thoughtful executive and I went on to have a fascinating conversation about the double power principle. If institutional religion has had great power for ill in our world, I believe that this is important evidence that it can have great power for good as well, in accordance with the double power principle. And, of course, the same point can be made in response to worry about other sorts of human organizations, like government, or the corporate world of business. If we view structured organizations under the governance of the double power principle, we see the possibility of fantastic benefits in human life as well as great evils.

At the time I am writing this, our sense of ourselves as a nation, as the United States, is still recovering from a horrible blow dealt to us all by the bombing of the federal office building in Oklahoma City. The double power principle is at work even in that tragedy: the fertilizer that grows the food to feed the people of Oklahoma was used to make a bomb that would take their lives and tear apart their families.

You can probably think of many other illustrations. The point here, of course, is how it applies to truth. Truth has great power for good. That is crucial. But what's just as important is to see that the double power principle applies here just as it does anywhere else. If truth is abused, if it is used in the creation of ugliness, evil, and disunity, terrible ill can result. Because truth is so powerful, it can be used to do great good or to bring about significant damage.

> *All cruel people describe themselves as paragons of frankness.*
> —TENNESSEE WILLIAMS

In the pages of the New Testament, the apostle Paul talks of "speaking the truth in love." I believe that what he means can be understood ultimately as an application of what I'm talking about here. The intellectual dimension of human life should never be ignored or neglected. But just as importantly, it must be exercised in connection with the other three dimensions of human experience. Truth should never be separated from beauty, goodness, and unity, but always, insofar as possible, presented in their context. This alone is a step along the path of human happiness and fulfillment.

Robert Townsend, former director of American Express and president and CEO of Avis Rent a Car, tells about a former associate who seems to have mastered the knack of speaking the truth in love. Townsend reports that every time he was pressing a new idea that this colleague didn't think would work, he would get a memo that began with the phrase "Dear Jefe de Oro," which he says is an Inca-like form of address, to be translated as "Dear Chief of Gold." The memo would continue like this: "If you say so, it will be my hourly concern to make it so. But before I sally forth in service of this, your latest cause, I must tell you with deep affection and respect that you're full of it again. . . ." Townsend says that this brave bearer of hard truth would then go on to detail the reasons he believed that the latest Townsend brainstorm wouldn't work, and that he was, as a consequence, snatched back from the brink of disaster by this concerned colleague several times.

> *Straightforwardness, without the rules of propriety, becomes rudeness.*
> —CONFUCIUS

We should all strive to create a context in which people are not afraid to share what may be hard truths, and are able to do it in as easy a way as possible. No executive can do without the well-informed feedback of his associates, who may be better positioned to see another side of a situation. No one in an organization can contribute her best without being both willing and able to convey sometimes difficult or potentially awkward truths in as positive and pleasant a way as possible. An ability to speak the truth in love is an inestimably valuable habit in any working relationship, and should be both explicitly encouraged and practiced by those in authoritative positions.

Knowledge and Power

In too many corporate contexts, managers and executives operate with what can be called an utterly inappropriate "need-to-know" principle, sharing with employees only what they are convinced those people absolutely must know in order to be able to do their jobs. But minimal knowledge is usually connected with minimal competence. What these managers most often fail to understand sufficiently is that very few people are capable of doing their jobs at a high level of excellence with only a limited knowledge of overall conditions relevant to their work.

Generally speaking, in corporate contexts as well as in life, the more knowledge we have, the better. Or, to put it another way, the human need to know is much greater in scope and depth than those who espouse such a principle typically seem to appreciate.

> *A man is but what he knoweth.* —FRANCIS BACON

The philosopher Thomas Hobbes (1588–1679) said, "Knowledge is power." And that's true. But a subtly and dangerously false proposition is often wrongly inferred from this, a belief that if you want to gain and retain power, you'd better gain and retain knowledge with tight exclusivity, hoarding and protecting it as your private property. Too few executives seem to see that the sharing of knowledge yields more than shared power. It typically results in greatly expanded power. The reason is this. An executive's power in a market, or in the world, is always to some significant extent directly related to and dependent on the power of his company, which is nothing else than the collective power of the people who work in that company. Any expansion of that power base thus expands the overall scope, or reach, of his own power.

In my own experience as a teacher, I've learned that when you share knowledge, you expand knowledge. It's not just that what I alone knew is now known by thirty or three hundred others. There is more going on than that. Every student with whom I share my knowledge is hearing and processing that knowledge from the perspective of a set of beliefs and experiences to some extent different from mine. The interaction between that newly shared knowledge and the prior knowledge of those thirty or three hundred other people creates insights that generate new knowledge beyond what I communicated, or even had in my possession at all. That's one important reason why in a good classroom the teacher can learn from the students just as they learn from the teacher.

The same point applies to the corporate context and to the issue of power. As knowledge is shared, it expands. And as knowledge expands, power expands. Why should you run a forty-watt company when you could all be blazing with light? Share your knowledge and multiply your power.

> *An investment in knowledge pays the best interest.*
>
> —BENJAMIN FRANKLIN

The Open-Book Game

This is the philosophical basis for the success of what is now coming to be known as "open-book management," an approach to business life that centers on the concept of sharing knowledge with all associates about the financial shape, overall market, and strategic plans of the company. Its name derives from the new and, in some circles, radical practice of "opening the books" for all, or at least most, employees, allowing them to read for themselves and understand all the relevant data on the health of the company. The open bookies are betting on the power and proclivity of well-informed people to do excellent work over the long term.

I had the pleasure of meeting briefly one of the pioneers of open-book management, Jack Stack, the day he was honored by the Business Enterprise Trust Awards for showing exemplary moral leadership in the corporate world. When he took over the helm at the Springfield Remanufacturing Company (SRC), the company had just been cut loose from the International Harvester Company, and the place was hanging by a thread, with an 89-to-1 debt-to-equity ratio. They faced serious problems and had no room for error. Stack was convinced that the only way to ensure that the enterprise

IF ARISTOTLE RAN GENERAL MOTORS

would work over the long run would be to make truth the foundation for all they did. He worked hard to build trust and a positive spirit in the company and finally decided that he needed to bring the big picture of their work together to every employee. So he taught everyone how to read and understand the financial reports of the company. He opened the books on a regular basis to make available the whole truth about where they were and where they all needed to go.

In his fascinating book *The Great Game of Business*, this innovative leader recounts the whole story about the role of truth in real workplace empowerment and the striking business consequences that he has seen in his own experience. It's one of the few books that I recommend almost every time I speak on issues of corporate spirit. Stack found that truth liberates. It frees people to be and do their best. If they just know where they are and what's going on, they can figure out how to do what needs to be done. Human beings can be surprisingly creative when they are just given the right raw materials and the proper opportunity. Jack Stack tells prospective employees that 30 percent of every job at SRC is learning.

> *Only the educated are free.* —EPICTETUS

It's long been recognized that working smart is every bit as important as working hard. And working smart is not possible apart from access to truth. Everyone who works around us as an associate or with us as a customer or supplier has an intellectual dimension, no matter what their formal education and current job description might be. If we respect and nurture this side of their lives with a give-and-take of ideas and with all the truth we helpfully can provide, we make an important contribution toward their feeling some measure of meaningfulness, fulfillment, and happiness in their work with us. And we thereby in turn create for ourselves a better environment in which to flourish.

2

Truth and Lies

> No man can be said to be happy who has been thrust outside the
> pale of truth.
> —SENECA

In business we want results. One of the greatest temptations is to do whatever it takes to get those results, even if that involves shamelessly manipulating other people. And, of course, the way we manipulate other people is primarily by manipulating the truth. By bluffing. By a little deception. By lying. In the ancient world, the writer Diogenes Laërtius reported in his famous work *Lives of Eminent Philosophers* that Anacharsis, a sage of the sixth century B.C. who had traveled extensively to study various human customs, defined commerce thus: "The market is a place set apart where men may deceive one another." It has always been the same. Truth is easily victimized by our desires.

But if you live long enough in this world, keep your eyes wide open, and understand what you see, you eventually come to realize that Seneca was right when he claimed that no one can be happy who has been "thrust outside the pale of truth." And there are two ways to be thrust outside this realm. One is by being lied to; the other is by lying.

Truth, Lies, and Sophocles

Let me take you back into ancient times for a few more moments, with a passage from a play written by Sophocles in 409 B.C. called *Philoctetes*. Here we find the famous and accomplished leader Odysseus in a conversation with his much younger, up-and-coming colleague Neoptolemus. Odysseus hopes to enlist this colleague's aid in dealing with a severely wounded but extraordinarily powerful adversary, a man who has long been an enemy, named Philoctetes.

NEOPTOLEMUS: Go on with your story; tell me what you want.
ODYSSEUS: Son of Achilles,
    our coming here has a purpose. Be loyal to it
    with more than just your body. If you should hear
    some strange new thing, unlike what you have heard
    before, still serve us; it was to serve that you came here.
NEOPTOLEMUS: What would you have me do?
ODYSSEUS: Ensnare
    the soul of Philoctetes with your words.
    When he asks who you are and whence you came,
    say you are Achilles' son; you need not lie.
    Say you are sailing home, leaving the Greeks
    and all their fleet, in bitter hatred. Say
    that they had prayed you, urged you from your home,
    and swore that only with your help
    could Troy be taken. Yet when you came and asked,
    as by your right, to have your father's arms,
    Achilles' arms, they did not think you worthy
    but gave them to Odysseus. Say what you will
    against me; do not spare me anything.
    Nothing of this will hurt me; if you will not
    do this, you will bring sorrow on all the Greeks.
    If this man's bow shall not be taken by us,
    you cannot sack the town of Troy.
    If, when he sees me, Philoctetes
    still has his bow, there is an end of me,
    and you too, for my company would damn you.

For this you must sharpen your wits, to become a thief
of the arms no man has conquered.
I know, young man, it is not your natural bent
to say such things nor to contrive such mischief.
But the prize of victory is pleasant to win.
Bear up: another time we shall prove honest.
For one brief shameless portion of a day
give me yourself, and then for all the rest
you may be called the most scrupulous of men.

NEOPTOLEMUS: Son of Laertes, what I dislike to hear
I hate to put into execution.
I have a natural antipathy
to get my ends by tricks and strategems.
So, too, they say, my father was. Philoctetes
I will gladly fight and capture, bring him with us,
but not by treachery. Surely a one-legged man
cannot prevail against so many of us!
I recognize that I was sent with you
to follow your instructions. I am loath
to have you call me traitor. Still, my lord,
I would prefer even to fail with honor
than win by cheating.

ODYSSEUS: You are a good man's son.
I was young, too, once, and then I had a tongue
very inactive and a doing hand.
Now, as I go forth to the test, I see
that everywhere among the race of men
it is the tongue that wins and not the deed.

NEOPTOLEMUS: What do you bid me do, but to tell lies?
ODYSSEUS: By craft I bid you take him, Philoctetes.
NEOPTOLEMUS: And why by craft rather than by persuasion?
ODYSSEUS: He will not be persuaded; force will fail.
NEOPTOLEMUS: Do you not find it vile yourself, this lying?
ODYSSEUS: Not if the lie brings our rescue with it.
NEOPTOLEMUS: How can a man not blush to say such things?
ODYSSEUS: When one does something for gain, one need not blush.
NEOPTOLEMUS: What gain for me that he should come to Troy?
ODYSSEUS: His weapons alone are destined to take Troy.

NEOPTOLEMUS: Then I shall not be, as was said, its conquerer?
ODYSSEUS: Not you apart from them nor they from you.
NEOPTOLEMUS: They must be my quarry then, if this is so.
ODYSSEUS: You will win a double prize if you do this.
NEOPTOLEMUS: What? If I know, I will do what you say.
ODYSSEUS: You shall be called a wise man and a good.
NEOPTOLEMUS: Well, then, I will do it, casting aside all shame.
ODYSSEUS: You clearly recollect all I have told you?
NEOPTOLEMUS: Yes, now that I have understood it.

This little exchange deserves a number of comments. Notice that Odysseus begins by appealing to Neoptolemus' sense of mission, to his loyalty, and to his sense of service. Then he sugarcoats the assignment of deception with euphemism and assurances of victory. The older man doesn't come right out and say, "I want you to tell a bunch of lies." In fact, he is careful early on in his instructions to say that, when asked by Philoctetes who he is, Neoptolemus "need not lie." Neoptolemus uses straightforward moral terminology here and calls the whole strategem he is being asked to undertake "lying" and "cheating." Odysseus, on the other hand, would rather talk about Neoptolemus using his "wits," about "contrivance" and "craft." Deception is presented as an acceptable and, in the circumstances, necessary strategy. Odysseus appeals to the natural desires for success and a good reputation that he shrewdly assumes will motivate this young achiever. And by the use of his own crafty persuasion here, he seems to prevail over Neoptolemus' scruples, further illustrating the very points he is making to his younger colleague. The end result is that he successfully manipulates one person to manipulate another.

As the drama continues, Neoptolemus follows the suggestions of Odysseus and weaves a convincing web of deception around their adversary. The goal is for Neoptolemus, whose identity is yet unknown to the powerful opponent, to falsely befriend and trick this man, Philoctetes, into handing over to him his very famous and supernaturally deadly weapon, an inerrant bow, so that it might be used by the Greeks in an upcoming battle of great importance in which they hope to defeat Troy.

Sophocles takes us to the point in the story where Neoptolemus has accomplished the task and has the bow in hand; yet here he stops short. A wave of self-awareness suddenly washes over him. He shudders to think what he has been doing and has thereby accomplished. He feels a great remorse and blurts out, "Everything is totally disgusting when a person acts contrary to his true nature."

> *The lie swiftly ruins the liar.* —MARCILIO FICINO

Neoptolemus then confesses everything to Philoctetes, who is understandably furious at having been deceived. The contrite young man humbly returns to the famed archer his powerful bow and implores him to voluntarily accompany Odysseus and himself to Troy for the greatest battle ever. Philoctetes adamantly refuses. Neoptolemus persists in reasoning with him, and ventures to tell him some difficult truths, but apparently to no avail. Finally, at the very end of the play, Philoctetes, despite all his protests and ongoing anger, is convinced by the voice of an intervening god to reverse his decision and go along to fight against the Trojans with his mighty bow in the company of both Neoptolemus and Odysseus.

One moral of this little story might be that once you've burned a bridge with lies, it may be that nothing short of divine intervention can rebuild the relationship and create a positive result. Neoptolemus acted contrary to his nature by manipulating the truth and thereby manipulating another human being. As a result he suffered an overwhelming sense of disgust with himself. The ancient philosophers would also say that he harmed himself by becoming a liar, an injury that he would have to work hard to repair. The object of his betrayal, the man Philoctetes, also suffered injury, although of another kind, and humiliation. Damage was done all around. And this is to be expected whenever, for expediency's sake, we depart from the truth.

> *Hateful to me even as the gates of Hades is he that hideth one thing in his heart and uttereth another.* —ACHILLES, IN HOMER'S *ILIAD*

The Price of Deception

All over the world, people tell lies to accomplish their ends—little white lies, desperate whoppers, ludicrous exaggerations, dangerous deceptions, tactical bluffs, and small feints. "It was shipped last week"; "We've never seen any such report"; "I've got some kind of flu, so we'll have to reschedule"; "I can't go any lower, we're barely breaking even at that"; "It just can't be done"; "Well, the problem is that there's another buyer who's ready to close now, at that price."

Who do you believe, and who do you doubt? When are you being dealt with honorably, and when are you on the receiving end of a manipulatively I–It transaction? It's a very bad thing to find yourself at the wrong end of a lie. And what's important to realize is that each end is the wrong end.

Adlai Stevenson is often quoted as saying, "A lie is an abomination to the Lord, and a very present help in time of trouble." Very funny, but revealing in its humor. Most of us condemn lying in principle, but too many of us still believe deep down that we really benefit from it on occasion. Paraphrasing roughly what Aristotle once famously said about anger, we believe that lying itself is not so much the problem as knowing when to lie, to whom, and exactly how much for accomplishing what needs to be done.

> *The reverse of truth has a hundred thousand shapes and a limitless field.* —MICHEL EUQUEM DE MONTAIGNE

Lying is one of the most dangerously corrosive and subtly destabilizing activities to be found in human life. When we depart from the truth, we begin to establish habits that can lead into a morass of uncertainty, a limitless field of shapes and shadows that shift and disorient like the reflections in a funhouse mirror. We begin to lose our grip on the truth and its importance.

Let's examine this in the context of modern business. When frontline employees see supervisors, or when managers see executives, lying for the sake of expediency to people outside the company, they realize, whether consciously or not, that they may themselves be victims of the same manipulative casualness with truth. There may well be deception *inside* the business. Falsehood cannot be set loose and then easily contained as a fence contains a dog. As Aristotle so wisely saw, action breeds habit, and habit can be very hard to control or break.

> *One falsehood treads on the heels of another.* —TERENCE

Whenever a group of individuals conspire to lie about or misrepresent anything, they create the most inherently unstable agreement possible among human beings—a conspiracy of lies. This creates a logical dilemma: You can trust your coconspirators to remain true to their agreement to continue in the lie only insofar as you believe them to be firm liars. But in that case, how can you trust their promises of complicity? Once deception is countenanced in the tactics of any organization, the seeds of self-destructive mistrust are sown within that group. And where trust is endangered, ongoing excellence is hard to find.

The roots of this connection between truth, trust, and excellence go deep. We are indeed all intellectual creatures. We have a natural need and affinity for truth. Even an evolutionary account of human life reveals this most basic adaptive mechanism: Those creatures who are not good at finding and holding on to truth die. A deeper philosophical perspective on life roots truth even more fundamentally in our created natures: Philosophers as different as the Frenchman René Descartes (1596–1650), often called the father of modern philosophy; Blaise Pascal (1623–1662), a great mathematician and early experimental scientist; and the Scotsman Thomas Reid (1710–1796), one of the great proponents of "commonsense philosophy," all believed that we are endowed by our creator with an instinctual affinity for truth, a connection made possible by the Divine Guarantor who provided this as the foundation for both sentient life itself and the higher activities of human community.

> *Speech was given to man, not that men might therewith deceive one another, but that one man might make known his thoughts to another.* —SAINT AUGUSTINE

Whatever your own worldview might be, it is extremely difficult to escape the conclusion that for human beings, at the deepest possible level, truth is extraordinarily important, and not something to be trifled with. We all come into this life with a natural bent toward credulity, toward believing what others tell us; otherwise, as young children we couldn't learn language, for example. If that innate disposition is denied fulfillment time and time again, if purported truths turn out to be falsehoods, if we find people lying repeatedly, then to avoid being duped we naturally become wary and suspicious. And when that happens with any individual or group of individuals, in relation to any activity or enterprise, our participation with those people or in that business is deeply hampered by the hesitancies of mistrust and disbelief. We are then always on our guard to the extent that it is difficult to be on our game at the highest level. Suspicion takes tremendous mental energy and time better directed elsewhere.

Once anyone has torn the fabric of trust, it is exceedingly difficult to reweave the pattern and regain that most important of qualities. Nothing will destroy corporate spirit more quickly than lies and deceit. That's why no one ever really gets away with a lie. Even if you aren't found out, you've harmed yourself. You've become a liar, or a worse liar yet. And to the extent that you believe you have lied and escaped detection, you suspect that the same is true of others, which harms your ability to deal straightforwardly with them and believe what they say, even when it's true and it's strongly in your interests to so believe. That's why liars find it so hard to trust others.

The Basis of Trust

Trust is like a lubricant for human relations. Without it, the mechanisms of interaction are damaged and grind to a stop. The only deeply prudent way to run an organization is to insist that people tell the truth, to each other, to suppliers, to clients, and to the government. Truth has to be one of the leading values of any organization that values its own health.

> *If the world goes against the truth, then Athanasius goes against the world.* —SAINT ATHANASIUS

I'm not saying that every truth needs to be told in every situation. Some things are sometimes best left unsaid. And I'm not suggesting that you shouldn't ever put the best face possible on something. But what you must do is always be true to your own deepest instincts about what the truth is and how it can best be used as the basis for your actions. If each and every one of us cultivates the habit of facing the truth and living in it, it will be much easier to share it with others, even when that sharing is slightly awkward or unavoidably difficult.

> *Be so true to thyself, as thou be not false to others.* —FRANCIS BACON

Respecting the truth, caring for it, and nurturing it in an organization is not just the job of top executives, although they should always lead the way and set the example; it is everybody's job. So as you interact with a coworker, remember the intellectual side of his experience, and as you deal with clients, recall their need for truth. No firmer foundation for ongoing excellence can be built.

3

The Truth About Excellence:
A Powerful Idea

A few years ago, I had an official philosophy T-shirt made up for my big classes at Notre Dame as a prize for top grades. Because I was once a rock guitarist, the cartoonist Dan Foote drew an updated picture of Rodin's famous figure the Thinker with a red electric guitar around his shoulders. This decorated the back of the shirt, surrounded by the slogan of my classes:

IDEAS ROCK THE WORLD

But in fact, this is much more than just a slogan; it is one of the greatest truths we can ever discover. Plato grasped it well. He realized that the objects and structures of our world can be seen as reflections of ideas. What we do in the world is a consequence of what we think. And how we do in this world is a result of how we think.

> A man's mind, stretched by a new idea, can never go back to its original dimensions. —OLIVER WENDELL HOLMES JR.

Consider the power of the idea of freedom in human political history. Or the impact of the idea of God on the course of civilization. The culture and life of any group of people, and thus of any organization, is to a significant extent a result of the power of the ideas at work in those people's minds—both the focal ideas that are talked about a lot and the background assumptions that are hardly ever mentioned, yet shape everything else. What philosophers sometimes call "presuppositions" are those deep background assumptions that form the rails along which our trains of thought and action run.

In this chapter I want to examine one of the most crucial presuppositions for business, sports, and even educational activity in recent times, an idea whose contours, depending on how they are shaped, determine the ways in which we approach work and interact with our coworkers. This is an idea that can dominate our thinking and divert all our efforts in one direction or another, based on how it is understood. It will knit together much of what has been said up until now in this book and illustrate the importance of themes yet to come. It is directly connected to the issues of personal fulfillment and corporate spirit. It is the idea of excellence.

> *There has nothing been more without a definition than Excellency: although it be what we are most concerned with: yea, we are concerned with nothing else.* —JONATHAN EDWARDS

This idea alone can determine the most basic dynamics of an organization, and either position us for the richest long-term success of which we are capable or else cut us off from what is most important in human life and most crucial for our own flourishing.

Winners and Losers

The word *excellence* has a simple etymology. It comes from two Latin roots (*ex*, "out from," and *cellere*, "rising") that together mean "rising out from." Excellence is always an actual state of superior performance rising out from an original state of potentiality.

But this is a very abstract understanding of the concept. Let me make it simpler by describing three models of excellence. It will be important for us to look briefly at each of these ways of thinking and appreciate their differences. There may be no more important presupposition for corporate endeavors in our time than the idea of excellence guiding our thoughts and actions. The spirit of who we are and what we do together can turn radically on this one focal point.

The first model of excellence is an inheritance from Western thought, from Greece, Rome, and the European tradition through which it has been developed. Accordingly, we can refer to it as the competitive victory model of the West. In this model, excellence is all about winning a zero-sum game. To put it simply, a zero-sum game is any contest in which, in order for there to be a winner, there has to be a loser, or group of losers. I can't win a game of tennis unless my opponent loses. One nation can't win a war unless the other side is defeated.

> *Every child of the Saxon race is educated to wish to be first. It is our system; and a man comes to measure his greatness by the regrets, envies and hatreds of his competitors.* —RALPH WALDO EMERSON

The rewards of any zero-sum game have to add up in such a way that the more you get, the less I get, or preferably vice versa. Envision a pie. The more pieces go to you, the fewer are available to me. In this model, to attain excellence in any given endeavor, I have to beat any others who come up against me. Competitive excellence is a state of rising from the crowd and receiving the spoils of victory. This has been the dominant Western understanding of the idea since even before the time that Julius Caesar famously announced "Veni, vidi, vici" (I came, I saw, I conquered).

The competitive victory model is so prevalent in modern life that to call attention to it as just one model out of other possible ways of understanding excellence might seem strange. This is a sign of its presuppositional status in our culture. Sports fans chant "We're number one!" or nothing at all. And, of course, Vince Lombardi, that icon of competitive victory among American football fans, is quoted in cities and hamlets all over the land as having said, "Winning is not everything, it's the only thing." Even our national governance is most characteristically manifested in politics, which is typically a race, a sport, or a competition, rather than an exercise in stewardship and statesmanship.

> *Man is a gaming animal. He must always be trying to get the better in something or other.* —CHARLES LAMB

Why have coaches and generals thrived as motivational speakers for decades? Why have sports and military metaphors defined the business thinking of generations of American managers and executives? Certainly, almost all of us were brought up in the competitive school experience of playing sports, taking tests, getting grades, and being ranked. And a great many of the people doing business and running companies until very recently—embarrassingly recently—have been men, and moreover men with military experience. Naturally, they have felt comfortable with talk of sport and talk of war. And for many of these men, the days of school play or even military service were the most vibrant and exciting times of their lives, the times they felt stretched to the limit and triumphant over adversity.

But it goes deeper. The coaches and generals of our day manifest some of our culture's deepest presuppositions about excellence. That is one reason they've been so popular and have flourished for quite a time as advisers and motivators of the corporate world. Of course, at least some of their popularity is due to their tremendous TV and print exposure. But this itself can ultimately be traced to the ways in which they embody the zeitgeist, the spirit of our time and the deep currents of our culture.

I'll readily admit, these men have some good advice. Gamesmanship is a mindset that can bring out the best in people, goading them to stretch beyond what they would otherwise attempt and sometimes rewarding them with an exhilaration otherwise difficult to duplicate. Competitive thinking in the pursuit of excellence can be helpful. But as an exclusive mindset, as the only way of thinking about excellence, it can become very harmful.

Problems of Exclusively
Competitive Thought

The competitive victory model tends to promote individualistic and adversarial thinking about excellence. Now, clearly, no philosophy is adequate that does not recognize the dignity and importance of the individual and sometimes adversarial thinking is just the kind of thinking we need, for example, when we are confronted with something we ought to resist. But a way of conceptualizing excellence is problematic if all the thinking it encourages is individualistic and adversarial in nature.

It has been well documented that individualism out of control and too much adversarial thinking has recently been pulling our society apart. A few

years ago, I did a videotape on the subject of ethics in the modern legal profession. In case you're wondering, it was not an extremely short video. I
interviewed lawyers of all kinds—members of huge firms, partners in small
practices, and individual practitioners—superior court judges, and county
and federal prosecutors. With one voice they almost all independently said,
in one way or another, that law is not fun anymore because it has become far
too adversarial. Now, you might think this a strange complaint, since the
very nature of our legal system is designed around a procedure that seems
inherently adversarial. Lawyers complaining that what they do is too adversarial might strike you as akin to football players complaining that too many
people keep running into them on the field. It's the nature of the game.

But that would be a mistake. It makes sense for lawyers to complain
about the contemporary practice of law being far too adversarial, just as it
could make sense for NFL running backs to complain that football has
become far too violent. Physical football must be, but excessive violence is
surely inappropriate. Something analogous can be said for the practice of law.

> Men must have corrupted nature a little, for they were not born
> wolves, and they have become wolves.   —VOLTAIRE

Some wise older attorneys explained to me that law was once viewed as
a profession of people motivated to solve problems for others, creating structures and resolutions and often healthy compromises that everyone could
live with, where winning and losing were far secondary to seeing justice,
warts and all, prevail. The exaggerated win/lose mentality now dominating
the practice of law prevents, or at least makes much more difficult, the sort
of civilized compromise that in principle offers the possibility of reasonable
solutions to difficult problems. The scorched-earth strategy that now pre-
vails has changed all the rules and created a new world of stress for practitioners at the bar.

This situation is not confined to law. A retired physician recently told me
the very same thing about medicine. What had long been a profession of
supportive colleagues in a community of science and healing has in many
places become a cut-throat business, where competition displaces concerns
over care. This was one man's report, but I'm afraid it would be echoed by
many others around the country who work in different facets of modern
health care.

People seem to fight over things very unsuitable for fighting.
—G. K. CHESTERTON

Clearly, in all fields, competition can often be very healthy. But exclusively competitive thinking can become quite problematic. In addition to encouraging excessive individualism and inappropriate adversarial aggressiveness, the competitive model of excellence carries with it one other major problem: This way of thinking about excellence cannot distinguish between individual excellence and what is most properly called competitive excellence. Let me explain what I have in mind.

As a guitar player, I am pretty close to my sustainable level of individual excellence. I have gone about as far as my talents will carry me, given my other interests and commitments. But competitively, I wouldn't sound too impressive these days. If I entered a top recording studio and was sufficiently foolish to challenge some of the studio guitarists to a little competitive playing, it would be extremely clear to anyone present why I am a philosopher rather than a professional musician. The point is, there is a form of personal, individual excellence that is not essentially competitive in nature.

We throw all our attention on the utterly idle question whether A has done as well as B, when the only question is whether A has done as well as he could. —WILLIAM GRAHAM SUMNER

But here's what's even more important. You can possess competitive excellence without having individual excellence. That is, a business or team can be the best in its league, or field, without being its best, as long as it happens to be performing better than any currently existing competition. When the competition is not particularly strong, you might be number one in your town, your market, your sport, or your industry without having come even close to realizing your productive potential. For that matter, even if the competition is strong, it is still possible to be the best without being your best. For a while. But this is, as you might imagine, an inherently unstable situation. Nothing ever stays the same, and if you rest on your laurels, one thing that's guaranteed is that some day somebody's going to leave you in their vapor trail. The only way to do everything in your power to see to it that a top market position, or a top ranking of any kind, is not just a blip on the screen is to do everything in your power to achieve your own individual excellence. This applies equally to individual human beings, individual teams, and individual companies.

So if your only thinking about excellence has been along the lines of the competitive victory model, you don't have the conceptual resources to see the difference between what is properly called competitive excellence and other forms of excellence. Your net will be inadequate for capturing some very important truths. And that's why you may have a blind spot to the kind of situation I have just described. If you want to avoid that dangerous vulnerability, you need a way of thinking about excellence that is not merely competitive in nature.

Unvarnished Truth

In my years of teaching at Notre Dame, I came to appreciate how pervasive competitive thinking is in our culture. My students would arrive on campus their freshman year having been at the top of their classes in high school, president or vice president of their student bodies, captain of one or two sports teams, the bright and shining stars of their neighborhoods and towns. And they got there competitively. Yet often I found that I had to point out to them that there is more to life than competition. I have professorial colleagues around the country who think that this news will be hard for some of our students to hear and should be broken to them gradually, indirectly, and very diplomatically. But I have always believed in being as straightforward as possible and saying up front what needs to be said.

A brief story will illustrate my point. You may have heard about the executive who is taking his first real vacation in ten years. The first day of the trip, he gets a fax from his assistant that states simply, "Your cat died." He looks at this short message in shock and immediately calls the assistant. He says, "Why in the world did you send me a fax that says 'Your cat died'?"

"What do you mean?" the assistant replies. "Your cat did die."

"But don't just blurt it out like that over the fax machine. When you've got bad news, for cryin' out loud, break it to a person gradually. Be more diplomatic. You've ruined my whole vacation."

The assistant asks, "Well, what should I have done?"

Our distraught vacationer responds, "Prepare me for it a little bit. I mean, you could've sent me a fax that said, 'Your cat's on the roof,' and then maybe an hour later one that said, 'Your cat fell off the roof,' and then maybe a little bit after that, 'Your cat's at the vet,' and then a few hours later it's more likely that I'll be ready for a fax that says 'Your cat died.' But please break it to me more gently when you've got news like this."

"OK, I'm sorry, I'll be more careful," the assistant says.

Three days later another fax comes. It says, "Your mother's on the roof."

Of course, this oblique way of communicating can be a waste of time. If you have something important to say, I believe you should say it. So I've always told my hypercompetitive students as clearly as I can that competition is not what should dominate their attention every waking hour of every day. In fact, many of the most competitively successful people in the world think of something else before they think of competition.

A Focus on Growth

And this brings us to our next model of excellence. It is well expressed by an ancient Hindu proverb:

> There is nothing noble in being superior to some other man. The true nobility is in being superior to your previous self.

This articulates what I call the comparative growth model of the East. Its roots are found in the various wisdom traditions of the Orient, from Taoism to Buddhism, as well as in that array of thought known as Hinduism.

In the comparative growth model, we judge whether we are moving in a direction of excellence not by vying with some external competitor but by comparing our present state with our previous state, our present self with our previous self. We make comparisons over time, diachronically, rather than synchronically, or at one and the same time, as in the competitive victory model. There is a form of comparison that is not competitive, interpersonal, or interorganizational in its application, and it is this which is at the heart of the comparative growth model of excellence.

I do not try to dance better than anyone else. I only try to dance better than myself.
—MIKHAIL BARYSHNIKOV

The comparative growth model is about development or growth, and what philosophers call teleology—purposive movement in the direction of a *telos*, or goal. Am I closer today to my goals than I was yesterday? Are we doing better as a company than we were at this time last year? Are we improving? How can we come closer to our goals? The new business strategy of continuous quality improvement is a current application of the comparative growth model to questions of excellence having to do with product, service, or process quality.

If personal or organizational excellence is the only reliable path toward truly competitive excellence, then the comparative growth model is a crucial guide for our thinking, since its focus is on precisely that—movement in the direction of individual excellence, on a personal or institutional level.

To put comparative thinking about excellence into action requires that we have a clear standard or envisioned goal, an accurate state of relevant self-knowledge, a strategy for improvement, and a scale of measurement.

It's no accident that I introduced the comparative growth model by quoting from a great religious tradition. All the world's major religions share a three-part ideological structure. They all lay out (1) a conception of where we are, (2) an ideal for where we ought to be, and (3) a path from the former to the latter. In every case, the overriding concern is improvement of our condition. Salvation consists in, or is manifested by, movement toward the ultimate goal.

It's clear that any turnaround artist in the corporate world has to do the same thing. He has to analyze exactly where the company is and what its fundamental problems are; he has to point out where the company needs to be instead; and, finally, he has to chart out a positive solution for turning things around.

Any diachronically comparative approach to excellence requires that we have a clear conception of where we want to go. What goals are we pursuing? What ideals do we want to embody? What are the standards to which we aspire? In my book *True Success: A New Philosophy of Excellence*, I stressed the importance of this sort of clear vision for effectively launching any quest for success. I think of this as the first of seven universal conditions for attaining success in any endeavor, and the leading step we must always take.

Also, any application of the comparative growth model requires a measure of self-knowledge. We can't compare where we are to where we've been without an accurate perception of both states. In order to appreciate our present state, we must understand where we are relative to our goal and remember where we've been.

> *All that is human must retrograde if it does not advance.*
>
> —EDWARD GIBBON

Next, we need a strategy for improvement, for moving from our present condition to a place closer to our ideal. It does no good to know where we are and where we want to go without having a plan of action to get us there, or at least to get us moving in the right direction.

And finally, we need a way of measuring progress, a metric suggested by, and often conceptually attached to, the goal of our journey. If, for example, your goal is to be the best salesman you can be, you need to have a good sense of how to chart your improvement. Do you track client contacts, degree of follow-up, effectiveness in closing sales, and referrals from satisfied clients? How is your learning curve with respect to your customers' needs? Perhaps you need to share with key clients your desire to develop a mutually agreed standard for measuring your effectiveness in what you are doing together. Comparison is always relative to a scale of measurement. Logically prior to questions of winning or losing, we need some way of identifying and charting progress, and it is the role of a scale of measurement to provide just this.

> *Forget your opponents; always play against par.*   —SAM SNEAD

Comparative thinking can move us along in the direction of excellence and the competitiveness we so deeply desire. But the comparative growth model, as our sole model for thinking about excellence, also has problems that must be addressed.

Problems of the Self-Absorbed

The comparative growth model, used on its own to guide our thinking about excellence, can sometimes encourage a narrow self-focus that easily becomes problematic. Of course, it's important for any individual pursuing goals, any company, and any department of a larger corporation to monitor progress and to aspire to improvement. But latent in some Eastern philosophy is a tendency to be unduly self-centered.

If all my thinking is about my predicament, my problems, my condition, my quest, my enlightenment, my final realization of the ideal, I can easily lose touch with other individuals around me. Their cares, and the value of broadening my focus beyond the bounds of my own progress, are forgotten. I can lose interest in structures, institutions, and relationships that do not obviously serve my self-defined goal, and I can unintentionally impoverish my life as a result. And what is true of me as an individual human being can also be true of a business, office, or institution. Insofar as the comparative growth model encourages self-centeredness, it can lead to a mindset and an avenue of conduct that, ironically, can be self-defeating.

Life is shot through with irony and paradox. I've come to believe that one of the greatest ironies gets at the heart of ethics. Let me put it simply in a twofold statement:

> Self-centeredness is self-defeating.
> Self-giving is self-fulfilling.

It might seem common sense that the person who is fixated on himself and on his own interests is best prepared to take care of himself, or that the company most closely focused on monitoring its own progress is most likely to make the most healthy future progress. Not so. In our world it is the person or institution that can look beyond narrow self-interest and self-monitoring, as important as these are, and see a bigger picture, contributing energy and time to projects and structures that transcend the immediacy of narrow self-interest, that ultimately flourishes.

Self-giving, it seems to me, is not merely altruistic in its results, however altruistic it might be in its intentions. In fact, the more purely altruistic an act of self-giving is in its intent, the less merely altruistic it is in its results. Simply put, by seeking to benefit others, you can end up benefiting yourself beyond any expectation.

Now I don't mean for a moment to suggest that there is anything wrong or self-defeating about a healthy attitude of self-interest. This, after all, is the foundation for any appropriate interest in others. What is problematic is an exclusivity of self-interest that never encompasses larger concerns. It is this that is ultimately self-defeating and ill suited to the human flourishing that we all so deeply desire.

We'll say more about this shortly, but the point here is that any model of excellence that encourages a narrow self-focus tends to blind us to what in the end might move us farther along toward the superior excellence of which we're capable. Thankfully, there is another model for thinking about excellence that does not have this limitation but instead can open up our thoughts and actions.

The Power of Partnership

The third model of excellence is one that I believe more and more companies and individuals have been discovering all over America in the last few years. I see it in health care. I've watched it develop in financial services. And I have seen it in industry. In honor of the fact that I first recognized it during my years at Notre Dame, in South Bend, Indiana, I call it the collaborative partnership model of the Midwest. It is a model focused beyond the bounds of the individual person or business, and it moves us in the direction of a new relationality in keeping with many of the latest discoveries of modern science.

This model rests on the premise that a person can be in a variety of possible relationships with a peer, and a company with a peer institution. These relationships fall along a spectrum in an interesting order.

> *I present myself to you in a form suitable to the relationship I wish to achieve with you.*   —LUIGI PIRANDELLO

The most negative relationship that can exist between individuals or institutions is the combative relationship. The primary stance of this relationship is fighting. The key attitudes, actions, and consequences of the relationship are easy to specify. They are aggression, resistance, and damage, respectively. Nations can be at war, and so can individuals. Companies can be fighting it out in the market. Businesses can be in a bitter struggle for survival. Unfortunately, sometimes combat is necessary in our world. But what is even more unfortunate is that we can easily take up a position of combat when it is not necessary at all.

Individuals, departments, or divisions within the same organization often find themselves in exactly this relationship when it is not only absolutely unnecessary but even clearly self-defeating. An adversarial mindset can creep into different component offices of an organization and subtly create a divisive spirit that benefits no one. In fact, it then often perpetuates itself until someone recognizes it as such, speaks up, and acts to correct it.

One notch over on the spectrum of possible relationships is the competitive relationship. The primary stance of this mode of relating is striving. There is no combat here, but there is a contest. There can even be quite a struggle. The key attitudes, actions, and consequences typical of competition can be summed up as rivalry and mixed motivations.

What I mean by mixed motivations is this. When you are in competition with someone else, you are sometimes looking at your goal and sometimes keeping your eye on your competitor. You can easily vacillate between actions that will move you closer to your goal and those that will just prevent the competition from getting there first, or at least from making as much progress as they might have otherwise. This involves a division of energy and focus that can sometimes slow your own progress and deplete your resources unnecessarily.

When my children were young, we lived next to a very competitive little boy. In every footrace down the sidewalk or across the front yard, he would run with his left arm stretched out to the side to restrain anyone who threatened to pass him. He would often expend as much energy holding back his nearest competitor as in making his own forward progress. And this, of course, affected how many races he was able to run before falling down exhausted.

Competition can be energizing and productive, or distracting and exhausting. It can sometimes even take on many traits of combat, in which case it degenerates quickly into an unhealthy struggle with many negative consequences.

> *What it lies in our power to do, it also lies in our power not to do.*
> —ARISTOTLE

Farther over on our spectrum, we come to the cooperative relationship. The characteristic stance here is agreeing. The key attitudes, actions, and consequences are acquiescence, nonresistant obedience, and a multiplication of hands to get the job done.

Many people think that this is the opposite end of the spectrum from combat. You fight, you strive, or you go along agreeably. But there is conceptual room left on our spectrum, and the next space is occupied by the true endpoint of possible relationships, the one which happens to be aligned with the new model I want to suggest for understanding the idea of excellence.

I call our endpoint the collaborative relationship. The characteristic stance here is partnering. The key attitudes, actions, and consequences can all be summed up in the phrase "synergistic interaction."

PEER RELATION	STANCE	KEY CHARACTERISTICS
Combative	fighting	Aggression, resistance, damage
Competitive	striving	Rivalry, mixed motivations
Cooperative	agreeing	Acquiescence, obedience
Collaborative	partnering	Synergistic interaction

The point is that collaboration is not the same thing as cooperation. Recall that I just characterized cooperation as a multiplication of hands to get a job done. Collaboration is a multiplication of heads as well. When you collaborate with others, you partner up; you bring the best of who you are and what you know to the table, as does your partner, and together you think and act in ways that might not have been available to either of you alone. The differences in your experiences and respective slants on the world will enrich immensely the thinking that results. At their best, collaborators don't think exactly alike but are sufficiently in harmony with one another that their differences create new insight, and each is taught by the other.

> When all think alike, then no one is thinking. —WALTER LIPPMANN

Collaboration is all about teams and basic transformation. It is about community, creativity, learning, building, and pioneering. A collaborative model of excellence sees this highly sought after human state of maximum achievement in relational terms. To put it in the most general way possible, in the collaborative model an individual human being, or an individual organization, contributes to its own excellence by its own actions, but the boundaries of its identity do not circumscribe the contours of its potential.

Synergy ideally creates properties which either do not or cannot characterize the related individuals alone who are synergistically interacting. I suppose a simple illustration would be to contrast the properties of water, H_2O, with the differing characteristics of its component parts, hydrogen and oxygen, neither of which, in their own natural states, are wet. Or compare the properties of a picture on a television screen with those of the pixels of which it is composed. At the deepest level, collaboration is not just one of many alternative possible means to excellence but rather an inevitable component of any form of excellence truly worth having.

More and more business leaders are coming to an appreciation of collaboration in recent years. But for many, it has been only a partial appreciation based on a limited understanding. There is a new focus in the workplace on teams. Technology is making possible new forms of partnership with clients and suppliers. And the concept of strategic alliances is gaining importance in many industries. But most of this recent emphasis is focused narrowly on getting better results. The deeper point often missed is that, properly understood and implemented, collaborative thinking and working can create more fulfilling and productive relationships, making for better and stronger organizations. It can usher in not just a limited improvement in how we do what we do, but a major improvement in what we are. To see this, we have to understand a bit more how collaboration is connected with basic human excellence.

The excellence of an object can sometimes be defined in functional terms, and other times in aesthetic terms. An excellent knife, for instance, is just a knife that functions well at what knives do; namely, at cutting. An excellent diamond is one that's beautiful, unflawed and perfectly cut. But the excellence of a person or organization can never fully be articulated in merely functional or aesthetic categories. Personal excellence is always to some extent relational. And so is corporate excellence. Our excellence never consists entirely in what we alone do or are, but rather always involves what we do with, or are, to others. In fact, it is the essence of corporate excellence to be collaborative in nature, and that means that at the core of corporate excellence is the reality of corporate spirit.

What is required for great corporate spirit, for the spirit of superior collaboration? Truth, for one thing. Beauty, for another. Goodness also will play a key role. And unity, as it is to be spelled out later in this book, is central. These are the bedrock of excellence in any organization, and of successful long-term relations between people in any context. And that should be no surprise, for they are also the most basic foundations for any individual human life as well.

Motivations for Excellence

I believe that most corporate leaders today are sensing that a lively spirit of collaboration is in some way crucial for moving forward toward goals worth pursuing, and toward forms of excellence that are sustainable over the long run. But in some groups I meet with, when I'm espousing the benefits of the collaborative mindset, I'm asked rather pointedly about how individual motivation figures into a collaborative picture of excellence. The question is sometimes posed like this: It's easy to motivate people who are involved in a competition and are thinking competitively about what they do. Nobody wants to be a loser. Everybody wants to win. But how do we motivate people if we are thinking mainly collaboratively about excellence?

> *All that we do is done with an eye to something else.*   —ARISTOTLE

The answer to this question will explain a lot. Competitive motivation is very straightforward. It's a simple kind of interpersonal interaction. I call it the Push. If I am running against you in a race, I'm pushing you, and you're pushing me. In an ideal competition, I'm pushing you to push me to be the best I can be, and you're pushing me to push you to be the best you can be. Each of us performs better than we would have apart from the competition. I've experienced this myself many times, and I'm sure you have too. One recent advertisement puts it in a clever way: "Competition is a lot like cod-liver oil. First it makes you sick. Then it makes you better."

> *A horse never runs so fast as when he has other horses to catch up and outpace.*   —OVID

There is another form of motivation connected with a focus on comparative growth. It is teleological, or purposive, in nature. I call it the Pull. This is the lure of an attractive goal, or a strongly desired good, recognized by Plato and Aristotle as well as by many other great thinkers of the past. A lustrous objective embodying a valued ideal, vividly imagined, itself inspires us to work harder toward its realization. It attracts us and calls us to put forward our greatest efforts. The greater the ideal, the greater the power it can have in our lives.

Collaborative thinking has it all. Its motivational support is, in an important sense, *the Partnership* itself. Its structure is twofold. First, as with competitive thinking, there is an interpersonal aspect, but in this case it is the encouragement of community. In a real partnership, in a truly collaborative effort, each partner encourages the other to be the best that she is capable of being. Each inspires the other. Neither wants to disappoint the partner. And each is there for the other, in bad times as well as good.

> *Good company is a good coach.*　　　　　—JOHN CLARKE, 1639

Moreover, collaborative motivation is, like teleological motivation, vision based. It involves the power of shared vision mutually developed. If a beautiful goal can motivate, a beautiful goal you had a hand in developing can motivate even more. It's one thing to go it alone, working toward an established end, and something else altogether to pursue a mutual vision with other people you work with and respect.

The intellectual and emotional pull of collaboratively articulated goals may be the finest example of what Aristotle called final causation, the lure of an end or *telos* in all its potential power. Aristotle distinguished four basic kinds of causes in the world that contribute to making things what they are, distinctions that for our needs we can very roughly characterize in this way: a *material* cause is the basic substance of a thing, the most fundamental stuff that goes into its being what it is; a *formal* cause is the form or pattern that makes something the kind of thing it is; an *efficient* cause is a force that pushes and in that way brings about something's being what it is; and, most relevant for us in this discussion, a *final* cause is a force that pulls, drawing something out into being what it is capable of being. To simplify and appropriate Aristotle's thinking, we can say that a final cause is, in a modern business context, a goal or purpose or mission or plan that, as an attractive end state, intended and desired because of its luminous, anticipated good, draws us on toward bringing it into realization.

There may be no straighter, broader road to the most productive sort of empowerment sought after by businesses today than the practice of collaborative partnership, with all its attendant motivational force.

MINDSET	MOTIVATION
Competitive	The Push
Comparative	The Pull
Collaborative	The Partnership

A Combination of Forces

Collaborative work requires taking other people's ideas seriously, treating all our associates as individuals with minds, with real intellectual experience from which we can benefit. Collaboration is founded on truth, for apart from sharing truth, no productively synergistic interaction is possible. To reach the heights of human excellence, the corporate spirit must be one of collaboration. Only then will the people in our organizations grow to realize their true potential in the greatest of ways, and only then will we reach the ultimate state of competitiveness we all seek. So rather than being fundamentally opposed to competitive and comparative thinking, collaborative procedures best reach the goals they envision.

In fact, even more can be said.

Lauren Patch, the creative president of Ohio Casualty, has pointed out to me that collaborative efforts work best only when they are founded on a clear sense of how the people and the company or companies involved need to experience comparative growth in order to flourish within their particular competitive situation. You can't just tell people to collaborate or to partner up in new ways, then expect something good to happen. Their collaboration needs to be guided by their sense of what their competitive context requires. It also needs to be guided by some sense of how they need to grow. And it is the leader's job to establish this horizon of understanding and guidance for any newly formed partnerships.

But no leader can do it all. The launching of new collaborative ways of working should itself be done, insofar as possible, collaboratively. The associates involved in collaborative efforts may thereby come to have a sense of the competitive context, or of the comparative growth needed, that could not have been attained in quite that form outside the dynamics of the partnership. So ultimately, in any true collaboration, a leader will be a learner, as will every other partner to the enterprise.

Collaborative thinking does not demand the abandonment of competitive and comparative thinking, but quite the opposite. The best competitive and comparative thinking require a great measure of collaborative thinking. And good collaborative thinking and working depends on the guidance of good competitive and comparative thinking. But it's collaborative work that is at the hub of the wheel.

When we contemplate the potential effects of an overarching collaborative conception of excellence, we come to appreciate the power of an idea, the impact of a truth, and the role of how we think in how we act. Ideas do rock the world.

II
BEAUTY

4

The Aesthetic Dimension
at Work

T ruth, beauty, goodness, and unity: four timeless values for any productive relationship or organization, the four foundations of sustainable human excellence, also known as the four transcendentals, so called
because they transcend, or range across, all manner of objects, shaping our
total experience of the world. It may be fairly evident on the face of it what
truth, goodness, and unity have to do with corporate spirit and business
excellence. But beauty?

Think for a moment about where you feel most relaxed, most peaceful,
refreshed, reinvigorated, and even inspired. Is it on the golf course early in
the morning? At the ocean, watching the sun shimmering on the waves?
Fishing in a river, shaded by a big tree? Sitting on top of a mountain, looking
down into the valley below, or over at the towering peaks beyond? Hiking a
trail deep in the forest? Maybe it's just sitting at a beautifully set table, having a wonderful meal in an elegant restaurant. Or, if you're very lucky
indeed, it could be that you have these feelings in your own home, or in your
own backyard. Chances are that, wherever the location, you've had some of
your most satisfying experiences of personal refreshment and renewal in settings of great beauty.

Why is it that executive retreats are usually held in locations of tremendous beauty? I give talks all over the country, and the higher the level of the
meeting, the more likely we are to be surrounded by majestic desert,

perched among rolling hills or craggy mountains, or sitting at the edge of a sandy beach, with a panoramic view of sparkling whitecaps and graceful seabirds. In our meetings, we philosophize in aesthetically pleasing and sometimes even elegantly appointed rooms. Why? Because these groups can afford it? Yes, but that provides what philosophers call a necessary but not sufficient condition, and thus an incomplete explanation. Even if you can afford it, why should you do it? Why spend the money on beauty?

> *The beautiful is as useful as the useful. More so, perhaps.*
>
> —VICTOR HUGO

I believe the reason is very simple. And it will direct us into a deeper understanding of one of the most neglected dimensions of human experience in modern business.

Freeing the Spirit

Beauty liberates. It refreshes, restores, and inspires. Most top executives know this and at least sometimes act on it. That's why they choose settings of great beauty for meetings of great importance. To entertain a big client, or to plan for the future, the best possible setting is needed, a site conducive to feeling and being our best together. We all intuitively know that beauty plays a role that can't be duplicated by anything else in its impact on the human spirit, freeing our greatest energies, liberating our deepest insights, and connecting with our highest affections.

Beauty is, of course, just one of the qualities that together structure what we know as the aesthetic dimension of human life. But it certainly is the most important. Ugliness is its polar opposite. I think we can best come to appreciate the role of beauty in human experience if we begin by reflecting just for a moment on its absence.

A couple of years ago, I made my first visit to Russia. I toured Saint Petersburg and its nearby environs. The nineteenth-century architecture of the palaces and other older public buildings was incredibly beautiful. But the contrast could not possibly have been greater between that magnificently ornate grandeur and the twentieth-century buildings and neighborhoods that rose under communism and now dominate the cityscape. At one

point I told my wife that, as a philosopher concerned with the human condition, I was lucky to be seeing this for myself, because I wasn't sure any
writer, however good, could ever describe accurately and poignantly enough
the squalor, the utter bleakness, the desolation of the spirit that extended
down long filthy gray streets; that lay thick in dirt yards rimmed by knee-
high grass; that screamed out in angry graffiti; and that took on a particularly
inhuman horror in massive facades, the lasting monuments to a stark and
oppressive ideology. No Disney World here.

What will be the toll of all this on the spirit of the Russian people? I
know that the Russians are strong, and it has often been said that they are
masters at suffering, but the terrible ugliness of rusted, stained, neglected,
and abused modern Russia is a challenge beyond any I have ever seen. The
squalor that I saw lay deep in the constructed world formed of soviet ideas,
policies, and habits—bad abstractions made concrete. In many ways their
urban blight is the result of a false philosophy, a legacy of old lies that they
are living with now.

When we depart far from the truth, we often find it very difficult to
establish much beauty around us. We sometimes speak of ugly truths and
false beauty, but these are misleading forms of expression. The two transcendentals of beauty and truth are most likely to be found together.

> *Truth is the strong composte in which beauty may sometimes germi-
> nate.* —CHRISTOPHER MORLEY

Of course, we don't have to cross the ocean to contemplate the impact
of squalor and ugliness on human life. Too many of our inner cities rival the
worst of urban Russia for aesthetic inhumanity. I have become convinced
that issues of beauty and squalor matter deeply to the formation of human
sensibilities, attitudes, and tendencies in early childhood. And they never
stop affecting us in later life.

Too many people in America, and around the world for that matter, live
and work in conditions of unnecessary ugliness. Even more live and work in
places where there is little beauty to be found. This is a damper to the
human spirit, a drain on available personal energy, and a threat to motivation and creativity. People cannot do all that they are capable of doing, and
they can't be what they're capable of being, if they are being dragged down
by a significant aesthetic deficit in their environment.

> *Everybody needs beauty as well as bread, places to play in and pray in, where Nature may heal and cheer and give strength to body and soul alike.* —JOHN MUIR

Certainly, there are heroic exceptions to this rule. There are people who seem to flourish despite the harshest of environments. But such stoic heroes in our world are few and far between. If we want to create environments in which people can be and do their best, it is important to pay close attention to the aesthetic dimension of human experience.

Beauty on the Job

Ricardo Semler, president of Semtec in Brazil, needed a new factory. After qualifying a number of potential sites, he let his employees decide on which facility they would like to work in. They chose one, and then asked if they could have a well-known Brazilian artist paint the new plant, including the machinery. Semler agreed, and in a very short time saw productivity increase quite impressively. This is an executive who had earlier involved his frontline factory workers in selecting even the colors of the uniforms they would wear. He seems to understand instinctively the deep connections between empowerment, aesthetics, job satisfaction, and overall performance.

Many corporate leaders have told me similar stories, on both a large and a small scale, over the years. During a visit to the Ohio Casualty Company in Hamilton, Ohio, I remarked more than once on their exceptionally beautiful floors, and was told by a number of the executives that this one bit of recent remodeling had lifted the spirits and morale of employees in noticeable ways. They even brought their families in to see the beauty of the building, and seemed to feel a new pride in the place where they worked.

> *Beauty draws more than oxen.* —GEORGE HERBERT, 1640

From the largest possible scale to the smallest, attending to the aesthetics of the workplace can make a big difference. One of the American companies best known for its attention to workplace design is the award-winning furniture manufacturer Herman Miller. In 1923 D. J. De Pree bought the

Star Furniture Company in Zeeland, Michigan, with the financial help of his father-in-law, Herman Miller, and renamed the operation in his honor. An innovator in home and office furniture design, De Pree also showed early on his concern for the aesthetics of his own workplace. As business began to expand rapidly, the leadership of Herman Miller decided that any new buildings they put up should express their philosophical beliefs about what human beings are and what we all need in order to experience the highest levels of happiness and excellence at work. As early as 1947 De Pree wrote that even in something as small as the design of a door, both practical and spiritual issues should be considered.

He had learned his lessons from a master. In a pivotal conversation held during the 1930s, designer Gilbert Rohde once remarked to De Pree, "You think design is the most interesting thing about a house." And De Pree answered, "Yes, I guess I do." Rohde countered, "Then you're wrong. The most interesting thing about a house is the people who live in that house. And I'm designing for those people." The head of Herman Miller got the message loud and clear and applied it subsequently to every issue of design he confronted. We should create buildings, design spaces in those buildings, choose pieces of furniture, array equipment, and establish policies for the use of these things with the people who will be working there in mind.

An architect for the company later summed up the Herman Miller design philosophy this way in his master plan for one of their buildings:

> How people feel about their workplace affects their morale and in turn their productivity. If we think of factory/office complexes as large, dull, strictly utilitarian structures, we fail to provide for the human spirit. Brightening the human experience and enhancing the environment is appropriate. The workplace should express a certain joy and embody enthusiasm.

This designer had it exactly right. Herman Miller people talk about playfulness, joy, and lifting the spirit when they talk about their buildings. Subsequent CEO Max De Pree wrote about his own work environment,

> I would like to have my office encourage openness and contact with other people—a friendly, warm place, not a countryclub atmosphere— not a living-room in a home atmosphere, but a place where there is performance—where work gets done in a warm and friendly way.

When it comes to the daily work environment, too many companies in the past few decades have paid more attention to their computers' needs for clean air and ventilation than to their people's needs for light, beauty, and comfort. And this has had serious consequences. One recent survey indicated that 70 percent of all American office workers were unhappy with their everyday workplace surroundings. By contrast, in a regular survey of Herman Miller employees some years ago, Max De Pree found that about 70 percent said they had originally applied for a job there "because of the way the buildings looked." Where will the best work be done? Certainly it is unlikely to be done by people who hate to come to work in the morning because of the plainness and ugliness that surround them. It is much more likely to be done by those who love their working environment, whose workplace inspires their enthusiasm and even a measure of joy. So I think it is no coincidence that when an issue of *Fortune* magazine listed the hundred best-designed mass-produced products of modern times, as judged by a distinguished panel of experts from around the world, four were products of the Herman Miller Furniture Company, and two others came from the Howard Miller Clock Company operating on a similar philosophy right across the street in that little town of Zeeland, Michigan.

> *Architecture is the art which so disposes and adorns the edifices raised by man, for whatever uses, that the sight of them may contribute to his mental health, power, and pleasure.* —JOHN RUSKIN

Not many of us are in the position of building a new facility, hiring architects, and creating a vast workspace from the ground up. But within the context we are given for our work, all sorts of simple things can be done to help meet people's aesthetic needs and provide a better place to work. Merely cleaning and painting a factory space, a loading dock, or a service facility can have a significant and measurable impact on employee morale. And I'm not talking here about a positive effect on the attitudes of artistically inclined aesthetes, but on those of regular working men and women. Of course, what's true of the factory is just as true of the office. Little things can end up making a big difference.

Tom Chappell, the founder and CEO of Tom's of Maine, told me that he had instituted all sorts of positive morale-building initiatives, from day care and profit sharing for employees to company-sponsored community volunteerism, and all to good effect; but the single greatest thing he ever did for company spirit actually took him by surprise. One night he had a dream about putting large, beautiful displays of fruit in the warehouse and production areas. The next day he told his managers about the dream, and within a week baskets of fruit were placed all over the company. If people got hungry during the workday, they could walk over and grab an apple or a banana or some grapes, and even if they didn't eat any of it, it was a beautiful sight they could enjoy. The baskets spiced up the workplace. Everyone in the company felt respected as a human being.

Within a couple of weeks, the employees were taking it upon themselves to go shopping and restock the baskets. They told their families and friends about this workplace innovation, and they felt proud to be working for a company that would treat its people in this way.

> *We are the children of our landscape; it dictates behavior and even thought in the measure to which we are responsive to it.*
>
> —LAWRENCE DURRELL

Rick Francis, the president of Francis Security Systems in El Paso, Texas, subsequently told me a nearly identical story, but with an interesting twist. He and his wife noticed that, about midmorning, their employees began getting up and wandering off to the soft drink machine, and then to the candy machine, for a little low-blood-sugar pick-me-up. The problem was that the high sugar kick they got would inevitably be followed by a crash, a sort of later-in-the-day blues. Productivity was undergoing wild swings, and the net result was not good. Rick decided, at first for purely productivity purposes, to provide a snack alternative in the form of fruit baskets, readily available during the day for all employees. He said that buying fruit in bulk for the baskets was very cheap, and he saw a difference in work habits and efficiency right away. This was exactly the boon he had sought, but the greatest benefit was one he says he honestly did not anticipate.

People who worked for him started singing the praises of the company to their neighbors: "This really is a company that cares." Nobody in the area had ever heard of an employer going to all this trouble for the convenience and enjoyment of his employees. Rick says that pretty soon, when people came in for job interviews, he began hearing that they were there because of the fruit baskets and what they represented. People wanted to go to work for a company that treated its people so well.

Trifles make perfection—and perfection is no trifle.

—MICHELANGELO

Recently, while extolling the virtues of the aesthetic side of our work life, I told these stories from Tom and Rick to a large gathering of company presidents. Afterward, a gentleman approached me with a worried expression. He said, "I really like what you had to say about corporate spirit and especially about the aesthetic dimension, and I'd like to follow along in the spirit of those companies you talked about, but I have a problem. We make fruit baskets." This, I discovered, was the president of Harry and David, one of the greatest providers of high-quality fruit and other gourmet products in the land! We first had a good laugh, and then—as a member of the Harry and David Fruit of the Month Club myself—I had to express my appreciation for all the wonderful food and service I had received over the years from his company. We then explored together briefly some other equally effective aesthetic strategies for workplace enhancement.

Aesthetic Surprise

As a professor of philosophy for many years, I have had ample opportunity to see in my own classroom the need for enhanced morale. One of my classes every semester at Notre Dame over a number of years was the freshman introduction to philosophy, Philosophy 101, a course taught to very large numbers of students. Now, these were first-year college students who typically had never had anything remotely like philosophy in high school. Over the years I could tell that the students would get very nervous in advance of test time, and so at one point I decided that for each of my three exams in that class, as the students walked into the room, there would be music playing, music to soothe their nerves and energize them for what was to come.

Before the first exam I would always play over the auditorium speakers the song "Don't Worry, Be Happy." One of my graduate teaching assistants told me the very first time I did this that it changed the atmosphere totally, into something almost festive, which he had never seen before on a test day. Students would be tapping their pencils on their chairs, with smiles on their faces, and would often be even whistling along with the music.

> *Music produces a kind of pleasure which human nature cannot do without.*
> —CONFUCIUS

One semester, though, the festivity did not result in very good grades on that first test. In fact, many of my students found themselves suddenly confronted with scores the likes of which they had never seen in all their school years. I knew that they would stay up too late studying the night before the second exam and would come in groggy. So on the morning of that next test, I planned to play, as I always did, the wild, rousing Stevie Ray Vaughn song "Caught in the Crossfire." That would wake them up. But I anticipated that they might be extremely anxious, beyond curing by even that rowdy tune, so I decided a little something extra would be needed. When they walked into the room, Stevie Ray was wailing. But then when the song came to an end, I just stood there silently at the front of the room with the test papers in my hands. Five seconds passed, then ten. The students began to wonder what was happening. Suddenly, all the doors at the back of the auditorium burst open and in came the Notre Dame marching band, or at least as much of the band as could fit across the back sides of that big room. They surrounded the freshmen and began playing the Notre Dame Victory March. The students went crazy. They jumped out of their chairs and began to clap along with the music. A climactic ending with the band members marching out of the room brought a loud, prolonged cheer to the class. We woke up the echoes and shook down the thunder. And I believe that it was as a result of this aesthetic surprise that every student in the room made a higher score that day than on the first test. Every single one.

One young man came up to me after the class and enthusiastically blurted out, "PROFESSOR MORRIS, THAT WAS THE GREATEST TEST I'VE EVER HAD IN MY WHOLE LIFE! HOW DID YOU THINK OF BRINGING IN THE MARCHING BAND TO PLAY THE VICTORY MARCH IN PHILOSOPHY CLASS?"

I replied, "Why should the band just play the victory march in the football stadium? Why not in the classrooms, where it really matters?"

After a second or two, a sudden look of stunned awareness crossed his face. "WHAT'RE YOU GONNA DO FOR THE *FINAL* EXAM?"

"I don't know. Maybe a flyover of navy jets?"

The point is, of course, that what I did for the class made them feel special. It made them feel appreciated. It made their workplace a place of enjoyment, to the extent that this was possible. And it gave them something to tell their friends. Just like the folks at Tom's of Maine, and the employees at Francis Security Systems.

Pay attention to the aesthetic, and word gets around. You don't have to bring in the Notre Dame marching band or have a flyover of navy jets. You don't have to shoot off fireworks. You don't have to hire a famous artist to repaint your manufacturing facility. A few baskets of fruit might do the trick. Or some beautiful plants, occasional flowers, or colorful balloons. Even fake palm trees have been known to help.

In truth, people in executive and managerial positions don't even have to do that much themselves at all. Encourage your associates to beautify their own spaces. Set an example yourself and invite others around you to exercise their creativity as well. Human beings have always had a natural tendency to want to surround themselves with little bits of beauty. And they will do so, if circumstances allow and the surrounding culture encourages it.

There are some very good books available on how we can introduce more art and beauty into our everyday lives in small but effective ways. I have found some of the books of Alexandra Stoddard to be particularly helpful in this regard. They show how little things can make a big difference.

> *The proper use of the imagination is to give beauty to the world . . . to cast over the commonplace workaday world a veil of beauty and make it throb with our aesthetic enjoyment.* —LIN YUTANG

When I was a graduate student at Yale, the Yale Health Service decorated their walls with striking modern art. Patients who were there for a few days with the flu or some other malady had a surprisingly attractive environment in which to recover. Numerous hospitals and other health care facilities have been discovering over the past few decades the healing power of various forms of aesthetic beauty. I personally suspect that we are only beginning to understand and appreciate the significant role that this too often neglected dimension of our everyday experience can play in human flourishing and organizational excellence.

> *Art is power.* —HENRY WADSWORTH LONGFELLOW

The Protestant Problem and the Catholic Corrective

As a Southern Baptist born and raised who served as a professor for fifteen years at a great Catholic university, I am in a unique position to offer the Catholic Church a bit of praise that can't be dismissed as insider self-congratulation. Protestantism often has been characterized as the religion of the word, built as it is around the altar of the sermon, a lecture of sorts that for most Protestant churches is the centerpiece of weekly religious life. A Presbyterian minister friend who is a trained theologian once said to me that the people in his church like to sing a few hymns, so he schedules two or three each Sunday, but he quickly added, "Then I preach for an hour and a half." This is the religion of the intellect.

The problem is that human beings are not merely, or even primarily, intellects. For this mainly Protestant problem, however, there is a Catholic corrective. Catholic churches, like some of their High Episcopal brethren, hit you in all the senses with visual beauty, great music, and performance ritual, along with the famous "smells and bells." You eat and drink at Communion, and have a full-body aesthetic experience of worship. The whole person is involved, not just the intellect.

> *Few people have ever seriously wished to be exclusively rational. The good life which most desire is a life warmed by passions and touched with that ceremonial grace which is impossible without some affectionate loyalty to traditional forms and ceremonies.*
>
> —JOSEPH WOOD KRUTCH

In corporate life, we are often guilty of the Protestant problem. We frequently deal with people on an intellectual level alone, and then expect to have the whole person enlisted in our cause. Or we give them the bare physical necessities for doing their work and expect it to be accomplished with machinelike regularity and precision. Human beings need more than that. If we want to work around whole people, we should seek to do whatever we can to provide some of what is needed throughout the whole range of their experience, including the aesthetic dimension.

There are many ways to do this, from beautifying the daily workplace to bringing festivity into the rhythms of our ongoing interactions. Casual Fridays have done a great deal in many offices to bring a new dash of the aesthetic into people's experience and thereby liberate their spirit of creativity and enjoyment. Playful posters, colorful charts, bright team T-shirts, lunchtime classical music—any number of small innovations along the dimension of the aesthetic can make a positive difference to the level of personal fulfillment, happiness, and thus excellence in a working relationship.

With so many people beginning to work from home offices or from the road, at least part of the time, the aesthetic factor must be taken into account in a variety of new ways. Where assigned individual offices have given way to the new process of "hoteling," or making available small private work spaces on a scheduled basis only, the beauty and comfort of common meeting spaces has in a sense become even more important. And the telecommuter working from home should be just as concerned about aesthetics as the office designer in the big company. Wherever you work, it's important to give yourself the aesthetic edge and engage the whole person. Higher levels of focus, creativity, and productivity will result.

> *We are lovers of beauty without extravagance, and lovers of wisdom. . . .*
> —THUCYDIDES

The Art of Work

The examples I have been discussing are all, so far, instances of passive aesthetic experience. But aesthetic experience can be active as well. Consider, for example, any performance art. The aesthetic experience of the ballerina or of the musician during her own performance differs in kind from that of her audience. The running back on the football field and the point guard on the basketball court are immersed in a level of the aesthetic not accessible to anyone in the stands. It's not so much that they see or hear anything different, although that is usually an implication of their greater and more intimate performance role. In the act of the performance itself, however, there is a kind of beauty that can be experienced only by the performer, from the kinesthetic sense of her own movement to the inner awareness of artistic "making," as the ancient Greeks might have said. The relevance of this to the business world is direct and extremely important.

> *Art is the conveyance of spirit by means of matter.*
> —SALVADOR DE MADARIAGA

We all need to experience performance beauty—active beauty—as well as passive beauty in our lives. And there is much opportunity for this at work. Not, of course, by putting on tutus or bringing a guitar to the office. But there is a beauty to be experienced in solving a problem elegantly, in creating a business structure, however great or small, however permanent or ephemeral; and there is beauty in providing acknowledged excellence of quality in a service or product. This is performance beauty in the workplace. Its importance to corporate spirit may be inversely related to the attention it has received. I believe Socrates was right when he said that the least important things, we think about and talk about the most, and the most important things, we think about and talk about the least. It's time we turn that around.

Is your work a dance? It ought to be. Is it a play? It's dramatic through and through. Do you see your coworkers as fellow cast members? Every day you're sketching, you're sculpting, you're quilting a pattern of interactions, of relationships, of solutions to problems. You are an artist. And you should be recognized as such. Likewise, you should think of your coworkers as fellow artists in pursuit of performance beauty.

> *The conscious utterance of thought, by speech or action, to any end, is Art. . . . From its first to its last works, Art is the spirit's voluntary use and combination of things to serve its end.*
> —RALPH WALDO EMERSON

This is part of what's behind the need for empowerment in the workplace that has begun to be discussed so much in recent years. People need to feel some measure of performance beauty in their jobs whenever it is at all possible. They need to be artists exercising their creativity in any small or large ways that might be available.

A concern for truth should continually play an important role in how we think about our jobs and in the many ways we interact with others in our work. But a concern for beauty should guide us too.

The Many Forms of Performance Beauty

The ideals which have lighted me on my way and time after time given me new courage to face life cheerfully, have been Truth, Goodness, and Beauty. —ALBERT EINSTEIN

How, you might wonder, can a factory worker be an artist and experience this form of active beauty if he has to perform the same routine motions over and over, all day long? This is part of the reason Jack Stack decided to teach everyone at the Springfield Remanufacturing Company what he began to call the "Great Game of Business." Even the factory-floor worker engaged in repetitive acts of assembly can play the game of business, using his mind to devise more efficient processes and motions, connecting his specific job with the big picture of what's going on in the overall company life. He may be able to see things no one else can see and make suggestions for beautiful improvements no one else could make. He alone may be in a position to create an elegant solution to a problem that no one else can solve, or even notice.

We need to encourage the people who work around us to think of their jobs in this way, no matter what their jobs might be. Everyone can be a performance artist and an important player in the great game of business.

Let each man exercise the art he knows. —ARISTOPHANES

There are many forms of beauty in the world. When we hear the word "beauty," we may think of different things. A woman may think of flowers. A man may think of a woman. Many people think of nature. Some envision a painting or a cathedral. Others call to mind a favorite piece of music. A mechanic may imagine an engine he's seen. A wood-carver may think of scrollwork. A luthier, of a guitar inlaid with pearl. A jeweler might vividly picture a many-faceted gem. A football coach can call to mind a spectacularly executed play. An avid basketball fan will excitedly talk of "a beautiful move to the basket."

Confucius once remarked, "Everything has its beauty but not everyone sees it." As a student of philosophy, I learned to discern the beauty of a well-constructed argument. Coming across a particularly ingenious piece of reasoning in my reading could make me laugh out loud with the sheer intellectual joy of it. A lawyer can appreciate a well-built case; a physician, a beautiful piece of diagnostic sleuthing. And for every form of beauty, there exists a form of art. We need to train ourselves and the people we live and work with to appreciate the small beauties all around us in our work.

Does the sales force appreciate the beauty of a great piece of marketing? Do the manufacturing folks understand the aesthetics of engineering, and vice versa? In modern corporate life, we often fail to appreciate the beauties of other jobs that, interacting with ours, are crucial for the life of the business. And that's no surprise, because too often we neglect to savor the beauties of our own jobs.

I think companies should get people together occasionally to talk about the times their jobs have felt great—those large or small peak experiences that keep them going or remind them of why they do what they do. A salesman might come to appreciate anew the real beauties of customer relations and client problem-solving as he heard a colleague tell the tale of his greatest victory. People in different departments or divisions could benefit from reading such testimonials in a company newsletter, even from people they never see. We need to learn to appreciate all the forms of art and beauty involved in what we are doing together. To fail in this is to fall short in our appropriation of the aesthetic for the furthering of our work. It is only when we fully appreciate and plug in to the beauty of our work that we make best use of this foundation for excellence.

> *Architecture is about the good, the true, and the beautiful in our edifices and landscapes, and physics is about the good, the true, and the beautiful in nature.* —C. WEST CHURCHMAN

The importance of the fact that there are many forms of beauty cannot be overstated. Beauty, as much as truth or goodness, crosses over the artificial divisions in our lives and in our work. If we can understand the importance of beauty, both passive and active, in the workplace, we can begin to take control of some of the deepest issues of human motivation in tremendously positive ways.

5

Creativity and
the Meaning of Life

I am convinced that the world is not a mere bog in which men and women trample themselves . . . and die. Something magnificent is taking place here amid the cruelties and tragedies, and the supreme challenge to intelligence is that of making the noblest and best in our curious heritage prevail.   —C. A. BEARD

W hat is the meaning of life?" A fresh-faced eighteen-year-old student had approached me at the front of the lecture hall after the very first session of Philosophy 101: Introduction to Philosophy. It was her first class meeting in the first semester of her college career. But she wanted to waste no time at all. She said she had just one question she wanted me to answer. And this was it.

I smiled and told her it might take until a little later in the semester for me to be able to answer her. We weren't likely to get it settled in the ten minutes we had before the next class filed into the room. Could she hang in there a little longer? No problem. But as long as she had the attention of a philosopher, she figured, why not at least ask?

As long as I have your attention, why not at least answer? Most professors, when confronted with a question like "What is the meaning of life?" like to mull it over, turn it around, examine its many contours, expostulate on what everybody in history has ever said in answer to it, criticize those answers, and reflect existentially on the remarkable proclivity of human beings to ask such things. You'll typically get, in response to this direct question, erudition, analysis, rumination, and critique. What you'll not get is a direct answer.

Well, the rules are different here. I believe it's crucial for our project—that of creating a new spirit in our work and establishing new foundations for our own job satisfaction and long-term excellence—that we understand something important about the meaning of life, so that we can root our actions in that understanding and guide our decisions by it. If you don't know the meaning of anything you're doing, it can sometimes be difficult to plan the day.

> *God gives us the nuts. But he does not crack them.*
>
> —GERMAN PROVERB

The Most Basic Question

We're going to practice a little philosophy together, to get clear on what the stakes are in dealing with the meaning question. So loosen up for a few pages, because business payoffs, as well as life lessons, will indeed emerge from our explorations. But to get there we have to take a short journey first.

Some people think that "What is the meaning of life?" is the most basic question human beings can ever ask. But there is another question even more fundamental than this. When you ask *what* the meaning of life is, you're presupposing in the form of your question that there *is* a meaning to life, and you're seeking only to identify it. But of course this presupposition itself can be called into question. The truly most basic query is more fundamental: "Is there a meaning to life?" And in answer to this, there have been three different positions taken by thoughtful people throughout history. We need to look at each of them to grasp the deep connections between business and meaning as well as their implications for our lives.

> *The meaning of life is the most urgent of questions.* —ALBERT CAMUS

Nihilism: Nothing to Worry About

Answer number one: No. There is no meaning to life. Sorry. Get used to it.

This is the philosophical position known as nihilism. In this view, everything is ultimately absurd and meaningless. The British philosopher Bertrand Russell is worth quoting at some length on this. He once made the following famously grim proclamation:

> That Man is the product of causes which had no prevision of the end they were achieving; that his origin, his growth, his hopes and fears, his loves and his beliefs, are but the outcome of accidental collocations of atoms; that no fire, no heroism, no intensity of thought and feeling, can preserve an individual life beyond the grave; that all the labours of the ages, all the devotion, all the inspiration, all the noonday brightness of human genius, are destined to extinction in the vast death of the solar system, and that the whole temple of Man's achievement must inevitably be buried beneath the debris of a universe in ruins— all these things, if not quite beyond dispute, are yet so nearly certain, that no philosophy which rejects them can hope to stand. Only within the scaffolding of these truths, only on the firm foundation of unyielding despair, can the soul's habitation henceforth be safely built.

I've always wished that he had added, "P.S. Have a nice day."

Nihilism is a stark and terrifying view of life. Fortunately, I think Russell was wrong—I should say, in keeping with the spirit of his views, dead wrong—in calling his bleak portrayal of life "nearly certain." It is no such thing. There is no method of modern science capable of discovering, as attested fact, that everything is meaningless. Nor is there any philosophically compelling case to be built for the extreme conclusion that everything finally comes to nothing. And that's a good thing, or else it might be tough to get out of bed in the morning.

Early in the twentieth century, nihilism was the haunting dread behind much existentialist philosophy. But there aren't many nihilists around any more. And that should be no surprise. As a practical matter, it's just impossible to live as a nihilist. Even the most hard-boiled negativist inevitably slips up and acts as if one thing has more value than another or treats one activity as if it is a more meaningful use of his time than some alternative.

Is It All Relative?

The second philosophical position on meaning in life that I want to mention is a view we'll call relativism. In answer to the question, "Is there a meaning to life?" relativists offer us a conditional affirmative. They say, "Yes, *if* you give it meaning."

This philosophy is very simple: If you structure your life around things you value and things you enjoy, you make your thoughts and actions purposive, and that is sufficient to endow them with meaning. A purposively structured life is a meaningful life. And that's all there is to be said. As the psychoanalyst Erich Fromm once put it, "There is no meaning to life except the meaning man gives his life by the unfolding of his powers, by living productively."

Notice that this view doesn't address the question of whether the whole of existence itself has any meaning, or whether all of life in the universe is meaningful; it just deals with the more immediate question of whether individual human lives, such as yours and mine, are or are not meaningful, and offers a way of making them such. I sometimes call it "The Do-It-Yourself Approach to the Meaning of Life." Crudely put, it says, "You want meaning? Then quit whining and give your life meaning. You don't need to worry about philosophy or cosmology or theology. It's entirely up to you."

That's the answer of relativism. It's a take-charge sort of view. From its perspective, meaning is relative to what we think and what we do. And this brings us directly to the world of business.

What do we do in business? We structure our thoughts and actions around things we value and things we enjoy. We create purposive structures and pursue goals within those structures, ordering what we think and what we do into determinate directions of positive accomplishment. This is precisely what it takes for the creation of meaning. In business, as in love, we give meaning to our lives by giving them direction.

> *The meaning of things lies not in the things themselves but in our attitude towards them.* —ANTOINE DE SAINT-EXUPÉRY

Problems for the Do-It-Yourselfers

Relativism has been an attractive and relatively dominant philosophical view in much of the intellectual world for a good part of the past century or so. It seems to offer a neat answer to nihilism without embroiling us in cosmic questions of daunting proportion. We can see to it that our lives are not void of meaning simply by giving them direction. But as a total philosophy of meaning, relativism faces two serious, and even potentially decimating, problems.

One problem for relativism came vividly to my attention one evening when I was on a panel about Woody Allen's films with a professor of psychology at a major university. Commenting on issues concerning the meaning of life that the films had raised, this professor of the mind espoused at some length the relativist philosophy and offered advice to the young people in the audience. He said, "If you want meaning in your life, then find something you do well that you enjoy doing, do it to the best of your ability, and you'll have a meaningful life. There is ultimately nothing more that can be said about the meaning of life."

A college student near the back of the room raised his hand and asked, "But what if I'm good at torturing people, and I enjoy it. If I do it to the best of my ability, then you say I'll have a meaningful life?"

Our apostle of relativism thought for a moment and admitted, "Well, there are some limits." But what limits? Where in the philosophy of relativism is there any room for objective, transpersonal limits? Why, in this philosophical view, isn't torturing people as meaningful as healing people, teaching children, or providing high-quality, affordable housing? Of course, we know it's not, and the point is that relativism can't account for this. Surely we *can* construct domains of meaning in our lives, but just as surely not all human constructions are created equal. It seems that we'll have to go beyond the bounds of relativist thinking.

But first, let's look at another problem. This do-it-yourself relativist approach is based on a general thesis about meaning:

Meaning is never intrinsic, it is always derivative.

For example, the sounds and shapes that form the words of a language never intrinsically mean what they are taken to mean in that language.

They must be endowed with meaning by intelligent, purposive agents (by human beings, or Alpha Centaurians, if there are any). The same is true of smoke signals, nautical flags, and anything else that has meaning in an unequivocal sense.

It follows from this general thesis that life has no meaning unless it is given meaning by an intelligent, purposive agent. And that's the basis for relativism. But it's here that we hit our second problem.

It's impossible to give something meaning unless we have the requisite degree of control over it. For example, I can't decree effectually that as of noon tomorrow, all the words in the French language will change their meanings. I have no control over the French language. Nor can I see to it that your life has meaning starting today. I don't have control here, either. And for the same reason, you can't see to it that my life is meaningful. Why? Lack of control. We can't give something meaning unless we have a sufficient degree of control over it.

It's clear that we have no control over the circumstances of our own births. I didn't decide to be born in the twentieth century. Neither did you. We couldn't choose the countries of our birth or the families of which we would become a part, and these things can make a huge difference in how we come to be formed as people.

We have no control over so many of the circumstances of our growth and development over the years. Who were your early neighbors and friends? Who were your classmates? Did you have any control over who would move down the block, who the teachers would be at your schools, what movies and books might come to have an impact in your life? Now, in principle, we can take charge of a lot more than we normally do. But life is so complex and vast in its details, and to a great extent we have to work with the raw materials that we are given. And I believe that the circumstances that come to us unbidden over the years have a major impact on who we are and what we do.

> *The life of man is like a game with dice; if you don't get the throw you want, you must show your skill in making the best of the throw you get.* —TERENCE

We have no control over the fact that we suffer in this life. You can't survey all the facets of life in this world, take note of the pervasiveness of human suffering, and just decide that this is one side of life you'll do without. We can reduce our suffering tremendously. But we can't eliminate it altogether. This is just one more side of life where we don't have complete control.

We don't have any control over the fact that we'll die. We surely can take some measure of control over some issues of death by living cautiously or foolishly, but it is doubtful that we will ever be able to attain the type or degree of control necessary in order to have death fall into the category of those things sufficiently under our control to be endowed with meaning by our activities alone.

What's the point of these reflections? Simple. If we can only endow with meaning those things we have sufficient control over, and if many of the most formative elements of our lives, including such crucial issues as birth, happenstance, suffering, and death, fall outside the sphere of this degree of control, then we are just not in a position from our own resources alone to endow our lives thoroughly and completely with meaning.

We can create islands of meaning within the seas of our lives, and this is sufficient to refute nihilism. But we cannot see to it by our own efforts alone that our lives are thoroughly meaningful, beginning to end. Something more is needed for that, which brings us to the third answer to the question "Is there any meaning to life?"—the view of absolutism.

Absolutes and Life

> My studies in speculative philosophy, metaphysics, and science are all summed up in the image of a mouse called man running in and out of every hole in the cosmos looking for the Absolute Cheese.
>
> —BENJAMIN DeCASSERES

If relativism offers a conditional yes to the fundamental question of meaning, absolutism assures us with an unconditional yes. Relativism says that there is meaning if we create meaning. Absolutism says simply that there is, objectively and absolutely, a level of meaning to life regardless of what we do, a level of meaning that can serve as a foundation and guide for our thoughts and efforts.

In the philosophy of absolutism, it is not the case that anything goes. There has to be an objective standard of meaningfulness. Any life constructed in accordance with that standard is a thoroughly meaningful life. And any life lived in disregard of that standard will fall short of full meaningfulness. Absolutism thus avoids the arbitrariness problem that plagues relativism.

Absolutism is the view most often espoused by religious believers who contend that there is an all-powerful God capable of, and actually engaged in the process of, endowing all of life with meaning, an absolute, objective level of meaning not dependent on what any human being does, thinks, or values. Since there is an omnipotent creator with power over birth, life, suffering, and death who infuses meaning into the whole, there is a completeness to the meaningfulness of our lives that relativism alone cannot capture.

> *If you want my final opinion on the mystery of life and all that, I can give it to you in a nutshell. The universe is like a safe to which there is a combination. But the combination is locked up in the safe.*
>
> —PETER DE VRIES

The problem most often raised about the absolutist view is this: If there is an absolute, underlying meaning to life, then WHAT IS IT? For many centuries, a chorus of especially religious philosophers have assured us that there is an objective, absolute meaning to life and absolute, objective values that we all ought to live by, but we don't find many succinct, direct accounts of exactly what that meaning and those values are.

The Absolute Answer

I was recently asked to speak on the meaning of life to a large group of very intelligent people gathered at a resort outside Dallas, Texas, all movers and shakers as practical-minded as they were reflective. I told them at the end of an hour of laying out the various philosophies, just as I've done here, that in all my days as a philosopher and all my previous years as a student, I had to admit that I had never heard anyone in a public place say clearly and straightforwardly, "The meaning of life is _____" and actually fill in the blank, offering a real answer to the question we all have.

> *In my search for answers to the question of life I felt exactly as a man who is lost in a forest.* —LEO TOLSTOY

I've never witnessed a living philosopher even come close to simply answering the question. Most have seemed just as lost as anyone else when it came to the ultimate answer. But I told my audience that day in Dallas that I had a first-year student back at Notre Dame waiting for an answer, and so I decided that I would come up with an answer, a real, stake-out-my-turf-and-stand-by-it, honest-to-God answer. I told them that I had gotten up extraordinarily early that morning and had thought deep and hard about it, questioning, analyzing, and pacing the room, when suddenly it dawned on me—I mean, the sun rose—and I realized I didn't have much more time to come up with what I would say. But I didn't need much more time because after the greatest burst of mental effort I have ever expended in trying to answer any question in my entire life, I finally arrived at the answer to this one: the Meaning of Life.

I was astonished. If I'm right, this is what almost all the great absolutist thinkers at their best have in some way or another suspected. It lies behind most of the great religious traditions. But it's so simple. I told my audience that day, and I certainly must repeat it now, that I find the answer almost embarrassingly simple. But it is a paradigm of those things that we insightfully call "deceptively simple."

> *What is true, simple, and sincere is most congenial to man's nature.* —CICERO

Some of the greatest wisdom in life is simple, but it is both profound and practical. Obscurity is not a mark of profundity, however many confused writers have hoped to bully us into believing otherwise. The medieval philosopher William of Ockham was right in his belief that we should never trust an answer less simple than one that will do the job perfectly well.

But what came to me that day could have been the sentiment on a greeting card. Now, don't get me wrong. I have no snobbish problem with greeting cards, many of which are extremely clever, funny, moving, and wise. But the meaning of life? My audience had flown me, a genuine philosopher, all the way across the country to hear something profound, and I was sure—

absolutely certain—that what I had to tell them would most likely strike them initially as . . . well, disappointing in its cognitive availability, in its rather immediate intellectual accessibility. It's nothing arcane or esoteric. So why does it seem to elude so many people altogether? And why did it take until I was in my early forties to present itself to me, and then only after a sustained burst of stunning mental effort?

> *Smooth runs the water where the brook is deep.*
>
> —WILLIAM SHAKESPEARE

Of course, at this point I admit I was reminded of my first experience as a high school student at summer camp, a retreat in Buena Vista, Colorado. I was with a small group of campers climbing a mountain for the first time ever. We were pulling ourselves up inch by inch, foot by foot, clinging by our fingernails, slipping, grabbing, trying not to look down. The minutes turned into hours, and at a certain point I was overcome by the feeling that perhaps I was pioneering where no man had yet gone, venturing boldly into the great unknown, risking pain and possible death to get to the top of a mountain in that ancient tradition of doing so "because it is there." In the midst of this exalted reverie and self-admiration, I finally pulled myself over a ledge to the very top, where I saw a sight I never could have expected: counselors dressed as Indians serving fruit punch to everybody.

Have we arrived at the loftiest mountaintop of philosophical inquiry only to sip fruit punch? Maybe, I suggested to my audience that day, I should keep my answer to myself. This was greeted with friendly boos and hisses. So here's the punch line. The meaning of life is—creative love. Loving creativity.

Yes, that's it. If you want to take a moment to get over any initial disappointment, I wish you would, because THIS IS EXCITING! THIS IS GREAT! This is the proper meeting point of philosophy, religion, and business. And my guess is, there are many people shocked that any two members of this threesome could meet. But this is the confluence of all three. The meaning of life is creative love. Not love as an inner feeling, as a private sentimental emotion, but love as a dynamic power moving out into the world and doing something original.

> *In order to create there must be a dynamic force, and what force is more dynamic than love?*
>
> —IGOR STRAVINSKY

Loving creativity. In business and in life it means the creative building of new structures, new relationships, and new solutions, new possibilities for our world that are rooted in love, a concern for the dignity and integrity and value of others in this life. This is the bedrock, the foundation on which any meaningful life must be built. It runs through the proclamations of the great religious traditions. It defines the lives of the saints. It's the attractive force within the scope of any genuine secular heroism. This is the absolute standard against which the relativities of our lives all must be measured.

> *Man is, above all, he who creates.*   —ANTOINE DE SAINT-EXUPÉRY

Relativism was right to believe that what we do and how we think are crucially tied up with the question of meaning. You can't just lie around the house, or indulge yourself endlessly, and have a meaningful existence. But it's from a place beyond relativity that true existential absolutes do come. And that is the territory of our answer. The absolute foundation for meaning in life is a kind of performance beauty.

From a religious perspective, the deep appropriateness of this is rooted in that ultimate performance, which is the creation and ongoing maintenance of our universe, with all its cosmic splendor. Our creative performances are then to be thought of as reflections of the love that brought us into being.

> *Nature is the art of God.*   —DANTE ALIGHIERI

What are you doing? What are you building? Where is your art? What are you creating, day to day? Is your life guided by creative love? In doing your work, are you somehow involved in acts of loving creativity? From the little things like speaking a kind word, helping an associate solve a computer problem or a customer complaint, or making that important return call even when you don't feel like it, to the big things like building a relationship with a new client, carving out a new business, developing a new way of working, inventing a new product, or creating a new market, what you are doing is building meaning.

And this takes us straight into the heart of corporate spirit. How do your coworkers envision their work? Do they think of themselves as engaged in an enterprise of creating? Are they aware that they are building meaning? Are they experiencing their work as a fundamental, creative part of the meaning of their lives? If not, you won't see the kind of soaring corporate spirit in your endeavors together that you're all capable of sharing.

> *Every calling is great when greatly pursued.*
> —OLIVER WENDELL HOLMES JR.

In business, we create. We are here for the business of loving creation. We are here to embody creative love. This is a high calling, and a most noble purpose. It is a calling and a purpose for everyone engaged in good work at every level of corporate life, and outside the corporate context as well.

We are all to be entrepreneurs of the spirit, living and working embodiments of the deeply powerful business of creation. Insofar as our daily efforts are seen in this light, they can be seen as meaningful ways of spending our time, and of using our most fundamental life energies. The business of loving creation is the meaning of life. And the meaning of business is, at its best, the very same thing.

Change and the Meaning of It All

A deep view on the meaning of life will give us a new perspective on that one thing which seems to be the most feared by the most people in the modern business climate—change. Rapid, even dizzying, and nearly constant change seems to be swirling around us in all sectors of our economy. Every industry is affected, and it's not going to go away.

> *For good and evil, man is a free creative spirit. This produces the very queer world we live in, a world in continuous creation and therefore continuous change and insecurity.* —JOYCE CARY

The pace of change may be at an all-time high, but the challenge of change has always been with us. In ancient Greece, the pre-Socratic philosopher Heraclitus declared that the only constant in our world is change. In the seventeenth century, the great scientist and mathematician Blaise Pascal said that we human beings are ourselves always changing, whether we're aware of it or not. He added that if he ever changed his mind about this, it would only prove the truth of what he was saying.

Change can be unsettling, and even threatening. For many people, it's just plain scary. With all the changes going on in the world of business today, some negative and some very beneficial, there is without any doubt a higher stress level in the workplace than ever before. This inevitably affects both job satisfaction and corporate spirit, and as a result, productivity.

> *Change doth unknit the tranquil strength of men.*
>
> —MATTHEW ARNOLD

In many businesses, a fear of change has become nearly paralyzing and potentially self-destructive. An insistence on doing things the old way, a stubborn refusal to adapt to changing circumstances, can produce a kind of constancy better known as stagnation. This is often the end result of a leadership situation that the economist John Kenneth Galbraith once characterized as "the bland leading the bland." Changing times are challenging times. But they should also be exciting times. They are certainly times that call for creative, responsive, and responsible leadership.

Change is most frightening to people when they lack a firm foundation on which to stand. If they have a strong base of unchanging bedrock values, they are better equipped to weather any storm. That's why the best leadership in times of change is clearly values-based leadership. When both employer and employees know that they share a foundation of basic values, such as the four ancient transcendental values of truth, beauty, goodness, and unity, along with the aligned values of respect, integrity, and trustworthiness, then they can move forward together with some measure of confidence despite tremendous change.

Human beings are comfortable with certainty, and very uncomfortable with uncertainty. You would think we were somehow convinced that the purpose of life is to be as secure, comfortable, and changeless in our work and other life activities as possible. But we are not on this earth to stagnate. We're not here to sleepwalk or vegetate. There is in the challenge of change something that is very positive and profoundly important, something that we all need to appreciate.

> *There is a certain relief in change, even though it be from bad to worse; as I have found in traveling in a stage coach, that it is sometimes a comfort to shift one's position and be bruised in a new place.*
> —WASHINGTON IRVING

Change is the condition for creative growth. And creative growth, in a positive direction, is the meaning of life. Therefore change is integral to the meaning of life. It is in itself no menace to be feared, but a challenge to be embraced, even when it's difficult. In fact, it is precisely in those times when we face the greatest difficulty that we have the greatest opportunities for positive, creative growth.

> *In the end, it is important to remember that we cannot become what we need to be by remaining what we are.* —MAX DE PREE

I recently read a remarkable book called *The Measure of My Days*, by an elderly woman, Florida Scott Maxwell, reflecting back over her long life, and I was taken by these remarks:

Hardihood is a quality supposedly created by difficulty, and I have always felt it to be a stimulating virtue. I like people who have it, and that must mean that I like people who have been disciplined by hardship, which is true. I find them realistic, not easily daunted, and they make few childish claims. This also means that the hardness of life I deplore creates the qualities I admire.

Suddenly I wonder—is all hardness justified because we are so slow in realizing that life was meant to be heroic? Greatness is required of us. That is life's aim and justification, and we poor fools have for centuries been trying to make it convenient, manageable, pliant to our will.

What I cling to like a tool or a weapon in the hand of a man who knows how to use it, is the belief that difficulties are what makes it honorable and interesting to be alive.

If we could renew our sense of a noble calling, not to settle into mediocrity but to strive for our own personal forms of greatness, if we could come to appreciate the meaning of life as creative striving with love, we would be preparing ourselves to take on a new outlook toward the phenomenon of change.

> *It must on the whole be admitted that there is a degree of instability which is inconsistent with civilization. But, on the whole, the great ages have been unstable ages.* —ALFRED NORTH WHITEHEAD

Confucius once said, "They must change who would be constant in happiness and wisdom." And it's also true that they must change who would increase in happiness and wisdom.

It's *supposed* to be exciting. This just follows from the meaning of life.

6

The Beauty of Business

The secret of life is in art. —OSCAR WILDE

I magine Michael Jordan in a world where basketball never existed. How about Jack Nicklaus, Arnold Palmer, and Greg Norman in a world without golf? Or Joe Montana in an alternate reality where football was never invented? Picture Bjorn Borg, Michael Chan, Jimmy Conners, Pete Sampras, Billie Jean King, or Stefi Graff without the game of tennis ever entering their lives. Think of Stephen Hawking, Albert Einstein, or Sir Isaac Newton without science. In each of these cases, a person became great within a structure that already existed, an ordered structure which allowed him or her to discover and develop talents and to put those talents to use for the good of others as well as for himself, adding to that structure in the process. Envision Picasso or Rembrandt without paint or canvas. Mozart or Beethoven without music. Downsizing king Al Dunlap without employed people. Just kidding.

Human beings develop to their fullest potential in structured activities. And that is what business is fundamentally all about: the art of creating, maintaining, and refining structures of relationships and activities in which human beings can grow, prosper, and live life to the fullest. This is the beauty of business.

> *Wisdom is the abstract of the past, but beauty is the promise of the future.*
> —OLIVER WENDELL HOLMES

Of course this is the ideal. And to the extent that a business falls short of the ideal, it's not a good business, regardless of the money it makes. The best businesses are beautiful structures within which human beings work, grow, and flourish.

The Basic Question About Business

We have not wondered enough about what business really is. Look how complex and all-encompassing this activity, or vast array of activities, has become. It's almost overwhelming. Throughout most of recorded history, trade or commerce has played a major role, but never anywhere as extensive, deep, and pervasive as the role it plays in the contemporary world.

Business has developed more rapidly than any other side of human activity in the past one hundred years. It now guides and directs nearly all our other activities. Sport has become big business. Science has too. Art depends on business for its support. The needs and aspirations of business chart the current course of our civilization and determine how each of us lives day-to-day. Yet we have not plumbed deeply enough the fundamental essence of what we do in the world of business.

What is business, anyway? Almost everybody will answer, "Business is making money," or "Business is the enterprise of creating wealth," or "Business is giving the people what they want," or even "Business is the engine of democracy." It has sometimes been said, a good bit more metaphorically, that "Business is war," or "Business is a game," and—isolating it from all other human activities as a realm unto itself—"Business is business."

The vastness, complexity, busyness, and stunning success of business in human life should be a cause for great wonderment. And since, as Aristotle believed, philosophy begins in wonder, business should naturally give rise to philosophy. We should be asking philosophical questions about the nature of business. Because if we don't understand the whys and wherefores of what we do, we can't chart our way forward with wisdom and insight.

Philosophical questions come naturally to us, at least in our early years. I remember the first time my son, Matt, asked me a philosophical question. One day, when he was three years old, I came home from work and saw him in the dining room with our old dog, whose name was Roo. He was standing over Roo and staring into his face, motionless. The dog's tail was wagging nervously. I saw them from the living room, walked into the kitchen, and looked back. Matt was still staring. And at this point the dog was glancing around, a little edgy and concerned over what might be going on. Curious myself, I walked into the room and joined them. Matt finally looked up and said, with a great look of wonderment on his face, "Dad—does Roo *know* he's a dog?"

What a question! Does Roo know that he's a dog? Does he understand that he's not a human being like us, that he's a pet, that we *own* him—or does he think he's just *using* us? A real piece of philosophy from a three-year-old.

Why do adults stop asking questions like that? Maybe because we'd never get anything done. Probably this is a good reason to pace ourselves, but not sufficient for abandoning the spirit of philosophical inquiry altogether. We all need to revive some of that wonderment we had as children and ask again basic questions about the world around us, like "What is business, really?"

> *It requires a very unusual mind to undertake the analysis of the obvious.*
> —ALFRED NORTH WHITEHEAD

The Art of Living Well

In his famous text *The Politics*, Aristotle wondered about the basic nature of human life together. Why do people live together? What's going on when human beings organize and structure their activities with other human beings, rather than attempting to fly solo through life? In particular, Aristotle was interested in understanding the workings of the polis, the Greek city-state of his own day; but more generally he wanted to understand something universal. After thinking long and hard about the polis, he concluded, "The city . . . is a partnership for living well."

Contemplate this for a moment. Don't we sometimes think of the city as just a bunch of buildings and people? We may even envision it as nothing more than basically streets and government. Or perhaps we view the city as merely a conglomeration of individuals and families and groups working and loving and buying and selling and stealing and killing and talking and shouting and . . . no. There's something more.

Aristotle found an ideal unity amid the great diversity in every city, defining it as "a partnership for living well." He saw the city philosophically as a collaboration, a partnership entered into for a purpose, the purpose of *living well*. Human flourishing. Human excellence. This is the ultimate point of having cities.

A city is obviously an organized grouping of people, however complex, a structure for human living and working. Does that sound familiar? Where do we first encounter an organized grouping of people? What is our natural first structure for living and working? It is, of course, the family. So how should we think of our families? I believe that a proper Aristotelian perspective would say that the family is also a partnership for living well.

Well, then, how about the neighborhood? Also a partnership for living well? Why not? But stop to think about it a moment. Remember my son Matt's question, "Does Roo know he's a dog?" I believe that at this juncture of human history, each of us needs to ask, "Does my family know that it's a partnership for living well?" "Does my neighborhood know that, ideally, it's a partnership for living well?" "Does my city think of itself as a partnership for living well?" Wherever we find that the answer is no, we can be sure that we're going to see problems.

Now we're ready to return to our question, "What is business?" Like a family, a neighborhood, and even a city, a business should be thought of as a partnership for living well. Business relationships of any sort should always be thought of as partnerships for living well.

A business is not primarily a building, or a collection of buildings, with all contained equipment, and it's not mainly a set of organizational structures or processes for providing a product or service. It is a partnership of people creating in many ways a better life for others as well as themselves.

I believe that employees should be thought of as partners with management, and all the people within a business should be thought of as partners with both suppliers and customers, partners ultimately for the common goal of living well. Ideally, those within a business should prosper and live better because of the business, but so should others affected by its activities.

Business Structure and the Art of Life

Now, for the most abstract, general level of our question "What is business?" The vast, complex array of modern activities known generically as "business" have something important in common. They are all activities creating, maintaining, and altering structures within which people can enter into partnerships for living well. They ideally contribute to the world structures within which we can grow, develop, and provide for both ourselves and others what is needed for living well. I say "ideally" because, of course, all sorts of things go on under the banner of "business." But something counts as good business, on my understanding, only in so far as it approaches this ideal.

The structures of business are, then, some of our most basic tools for the performance art of life. This is the beauty of business. The beauty of what it can be, and what it should be. And this is the art of business: the art of creating structures within which human partnerships can flourish, partnerships for living well.

If Aristotle ran General Motors, everyone employed there would think of it as one huge partnership, encompassing myriads of smaller partnerships, for the purpose of living well. If he ran the corner grocery, he would instill in everyone there the same mindset. And if he offered you advice, I think that this would be at its core: Always think of yourself as entering with other people into partnerships for living well. This highly general truth about the deep beauty of business can provide us with an important perspective on many specific decisions we face. We should always be asking ourselves whether what we contemplate doing will enhance or diminish this crucial function of the business within our own domain of influence. Are we building partnerships for living well?

By developing, maintaining, refining, extending, and improving business structures, on whatever scale, we give people the means of discovering, developing, and utilizing their innate talents. We help the people who work with us grow. We can even help them to become stars, and superstars, the Michael Jordans of sales and shipping, accounting and customer service.

And we can help all those who benefit from our activities—our suppliers, our customers, and our communities—grow as well.

What then is business? Business is the art of growth. Growth is the essence of life. And so our answer quickly follows. Business is the art of life.

> *I want to help you to grow as beautiful as God meant you to be when He thought of you first.*　　　　—GEORGE MACDONALD

If every executive, every manager, and every worker could adopt the attitude expressed by theological novelist George Macdonald, the world of work would be a very different place from the one most people now experience. It would be a place for pursuing the art of life, and the art of living well.

Humane Business and Human Good

Following Aristotle, and weaving in an important element of the Judeo-Christian tradition of thought, I believe we can conceive of an altogether general formula for human good at the highest level:

PEOPLE IN PARTNERSHIP FOR A SHARED PURPOSE

A few brief comments on each part of this formula are in order. Ideally, whenever people are in a productive partnership together, they need to share purposes which are rooted in their deepest values and have been arrived at through a process of at least some mutual exploration and development. The partnership should be a true collaboration, with the active engagement of all parties bringing the best of who they are, what they know, and what they can do to that collaboration, and with both respect and honor flowing from each partner to each other partner. The people involved should be acting ethically, and should be showing each other love and appreciation as they interact.

Paul Singer, the founder and retired president of Paul Singer Floor Coverings in southern California, which is now a major part of MSA Industries, the dominant force in its market, is a man of great insight. On two different occasions, over a period of about six days, I watched him interact with a large national sales force at annual meetings. He couldn't walk into a room without getting hugged by six people within the first minute or so. And in conversation with employees he hired years ago, I heard superlative after superlative thrown his way. I finally asked him the secret of his palpable appeal. How did he build up such an impressive organization of bright, articulate, energetic, and enthusiastic people? And how could I get hugs like that when I walk into a room?

"You gotta treat people with love and appreciation," he said. "Love and appreciation." A phrase that until then I had never heard from a CEO or any other executive. It struck me right away that, after the publication of his massive *Principles of Human Psychology* in 1890, the prominent Harvard philosopher and psychologist William James had once said that his most serious omission in that great work was his failure to realize that the single greatest source of human motivation is the need to be appreciated.

In a seminar with about fifty sports administrators from around the country, I once had an extremely illuminating experience. Near the end of a session on success in the workplace, I put a blank transparency on the overhead projector I was using and drew a vertical line down the middle of the sheet of clear plastic. I wrote at the top of the left column, "Buzzwords of Business Success." Then I said to the assembled group, "Give me some modern-day buzzwords of business success, anybody." Immediately, people started shouting out things like "leadership," "empowerment," "quality," "service," and "reengineering." It was like popcorn popping. I wrote as fast as I could, putting all these terms in a vertical column on the overhead, until we had over a dozen on the screen.

Then I covered up our list, leaving only the right side of the transparency, still blank, to be projected onto the screen. At the top of this side I wrote, "Ideal Friendship and Family Life." I invited the group to give me characteristics that make for good friendship and family life. No takers. The room was silent. I redescribed the category. "What qualities do we need, what attributes should we display, to have strong families and friendships?" Nothing. People who just minutes before were yelling out things like "maximization" were suddenly mute. You would have thought everybody in the room had been born and raised in B-school rather than in a family. "Come on!" I urged. "I've got a candy bar for any good suggestion." At this, a man halfway back in the room hesitantly raised his hand and offered in a very uncertain voice, "Love?"

"Yes! Love!" I shouted while tossing him a Snickers bar. "Good answer!" I ignored his tentative tone and implored the group to give me another characteristic needed for good friendship and family life. A woman said, "Appreciation?"

"Yes! Appreciation!" I wrote the word right under *"love."* Confidence began to build at this point and, one by one, although still a bit slowly, I got *"forgiveness," "nurture,"* and *"respect."* The list then continued to grow until we eventually had about the same number of words as on our first list. I pulled off the masking paper hiding the first column, and we looked at both lists side by side.

BUZZWORDS OF BUSINESS SUCCESS	IDEAL FRIENDSHIP AND FAMILY LIFE
Leadership	Love
Empowerment	Appreciation
Quality	Forgiveness
Service	Nurture
Followership	Respect
Maximization	Support
TQM	Understanding
Reengineering	Sympathy
Ownership	Giving
Teamwork	Communication
Intrapreneuring	Care
Learning organizations	Trust
Focus	Honesty

It didn't take more than a few seconds for something to jump out at us. Someone pointed out that there was not a single word on both sides of the list. We let this sink in for a minute. It taught us an important lesson that we all went on to discuss at length.

The New Neighborhood at Work

The people we see at work each day, the people around us whose thoughts and activities will be largely responsible for whether we all experience business success together, are all people who come from families, and are all people who need friendship in their lives. However, how many people come from ideal family backgrounds? If you read current magazines, listen to a little neighborhood and workplace gossip, and especially if you watch daytime TV talk shows, you've come to a new understanding of the word *dysfunctional*. The nuclear family, that immediate grouping of parents and children, is experiencing stresses and fragmentations on a level not reached before in modern times. And how many of us enjoy the comforts of an extended family? For most of my married life, I have lived a thousand miles from any relatives, and so has my wife. Our society is characterized by tremendous mobility. It's rare for most of us these days to enjoy what people have experienced as a matter of course throughout the majority of human history, even up until the last few decades: We don't grow up around grandparents and down the street, or at least across town, from aunts, uncles, and cousins.

Think about this. For all of human history, something like a neighborhood has mattered greatly, from the earliest days of the tribe and the tribal village. Even within nomadic groups, there were close communities of people who would move together, in a sense taking the neighborhood with them to a new locale. Watch old movies and talk to elderly relatives (over the phone, most likely) and you can both see and hear things about neighborhood that seem to be ancient history. In executive residential areas, you'll often notice For Sale signs every few houses. People rarely know their neighbors. You may have waved at the family down the block, or at the guy across the street when he was out mowing his grass, back before he got the lawn service, but chances are, especially if you live in a white-collar area, you don't know the people up and down the street like folks used to know their neighbors. So what's the problem in modern America? Are the residential avenues filled with alligators and land mines? Why won't people cross the street to meet their neighbors?

This is a great loss. A young man at Notre Dame who hailed from a very small town in the Midwest, where the past still lives on, explained to me why he never got in any real trouble growing up. He said, "I knew that if I ever did anything wrong in my home town, six people would whip me before my mother even found out about it."

I was reminded of the old and nowadays familiar African proverb, "It takes a village to raise a child." Discipline, comfort, a sense of belonging, a feeling of connectedness, wisdom from across the generations—every human being needs these things.

> *It seems to me that our value system and world view should be as closely integrated into our work lives as they are integrated into our lives with our families, our churches, and our other activities and groups.* —MAX DE PREE

In a remarkable book called *Love and Profit: The Art of Caring Leadership*, James Autry, former president of the Meredith Publishing Group, draws our attention to these same issues and makes an important point. Most people these days, he says, seem to spend the majority of their waking hours at work. When you think about it, it begins to look as if the workplace is the new neighborhood. The workplace is the new extended family—or at least it could be. Autry believes that contemporary businesses now have an opportunity that has never before existed in quite the same way in the realm of commerce, to create a new kind of workplace fulfillment and workplace loyalty by meeting many of the deep human needs that are no longer being met through traditional means: needs for love and appreciation, needs for respect and forgiveness and nurture and support.

I was in Taos, New Mexico, not long ago, on a retreat with a remarkable group of company presidents from the West Coast, representing a great diversity of businesses. Again, I put up the two-column chart and asked their views on this split between the personal and the professional. There seemed to be a quick consensus that the things referred to on the left side, by the buzzwords of business success, could never have the results we hope for without being rooted in the things referred to by the terms on the right side of our chart, the genuinely human array of personal attributes.

Teamwork, for example, must be rooted in genuine respect and understanding. Leadership must be grounded in love and appreciation. And without the whole list on the right, reengineering is mere tinkering that sometimes takes us, in the words of the ancient theologian Tertullian, "out of the frying pan into the fire." Neglect of what is genuinely human is the major reason why so many people in American business right now feel more victimized than helped by the latest management techniques and companywide processes for improvement.

And yet for all the ink spilled over the items on the left-hand side of our list, how much do we read in the business press about the genuinely human needs on the right? Has the *Harvard Business Review* ever explored the role of forgiveness in human life, and thus in corporate life? Not to my knowledge. These are said to be the "soft issues," the unquantifiable and, thanks to some of the excesses of the sixties and seventies, "touchy-feely" issues. Baloney. These are the genuinely human issues. The humane issues. And as long as human beings do the work, make the deals, use the products, buy the services, and chart the future, these should be the most important issues, not the most ignored.

The Beauty of Business and the Artistry of Life

The beauty of business is that within its structures these human needs can be addressed with great power and great results—if we keep them in focus. If they provide the core of our big picture and the structure for our work. Then we have coordinates on our map worth steering by, standards by which to check ourselves and guide our decisions.

The beauty of business is, finally, the artistry of life. A major strand of the aesthetic dimension of human life is the performance and active experience of meaningful creation. And that's one reason deeply rooted in human nature why empowering people, pushing a creative scope for decision making as far down the corporate hierarchy as possible into the front lines, is so important. People will not feel fulfilled in what they do, and will not be experiencing that measure of personal happiness they are capable of attaining on the job unless they are feeling that the aesthetic dimension of their experience is being respected and nurtured by the people around them and by the conditions of their work.

We all have to contribute in our own ways toward providing the proper soil and nutrients for human beings to grow as people, and to develop as artists themselves at work. And this is true at every level of corporate life. Even the smallest job can provide a palette and canvas for real human artistry.

> *A great artist can paint a great picture on a small canvas.*
>
> —C. D. WARNER

We should never forget that a concern for the aesthetic is everybody's business. Everyone in each of our business environments should be a partner for living well. The beauty and artistry of the workplace is everybody's business. And in this way, reinventing corporate spirit and reestablishing a new foundation for sustainable excellence in modern business is everybody's job.

III
GOODNESS

7

The Moral Dimension
at Work

The third universal dimension of human experience is the moral dimension, that aspect of our nature that strives for goodness. This may be the most misunderstood of all four basic dimensions of human life. It is also, and not by coincidence, one of the most unappreciated in business matters.

Misunderstanding Ethics

Several years ago, when I was first asked as a philosopher to go out into the broader business community and give talks on ethics, I decided to find out what contemporary businesspeople were reading, hearing, and saying about ethical issues. I read magazine articles, professional journals, and popular books. I watched videos and listened to audiotapes. I worked my way through all the best-known motivational material. And I also decided to consult all the current quotations dictionaries to see what other speakers on ethics might be saying when they addressed the topic.

My greatest surprise came as I thumbed through these quotation guides, looking up such topics as "ethics," "morality," "good," "evil," and "virtue." A significant percentage, sometimes even a majority, of the quotations I came across were in one way or another negative, cynical, or dismissive. Sometimes, admittedly, they were very funny—like Mae West's famous remark that whenever she was forced to choose between two evils, she liked to try the one she'd never tried before; or Woody Allen's view that "good people seem to sleep better at night, but bad people appear to enjoy their waking hours more." Clever, but telling.

Why did so many quotes about morality or ethics convey such a negative attitude? One of the most important reasons is that for a long time, too many people seem to have misunderstood what ethics is all about. They think that ethics is about restriction and constraint, about not being allowed to do what we might otherwise really enjoy doing, perhaps for the reason of social control, or so as not to offend the more sanctimonious among us. Until we shake ourselves free of this illusion, we will not appreciate one of the most important foundations for positive corporate spirit and sustainable success in our work.

What Moral Goodness Is All About

We human beings need goodness in our lives every bit as much as we need truth or beauty. In fact, there are deep connections among these three transcendentals. It has been said that truth is among the greatest beauties, and that beauty is the deepest truth of our world. We might be led to wonder whether this is just poetry or fact. The poet John Keats proclaimed, "What the imagination seizes as beauty must be truth." But many mathematicians and physicists seem to concur, as they uncover hints of intellectual elegance in the most hidden truths of our world.

> *Goodness is a special kind of truth and beauty. It is truth and beauty in human behavior.* —H. A. OVERSTREET

The philosopher Jean-Jacques Rousseau once stated, "I have always believed that good is only beauty put into practice." And to my mind, it is undeniable that one of the most common ways of departing from goodness is departing from truth.

Like truth and beauty, goodness is the soil within which the soul can grow and flourish. Without it, human beings wither and harden and spiritually die. Goodness is a necessary condition for healthy relationships and for thriving community. Morality is not about deprivation, denial, and artificial constraint; quite to the contrary, it is about ultimately living as well as human beings are capable of living.

What's in It For Me?

In the classroom, professors who talk about moral issues sometimes hear a very blunt question that most polite people are usually loathe to raise when ethics is being discussed in public—although many may think it—"What's in it for me?" When this question is asked about morality it can seem especially perverse. It seems almost a caricature of an amoral perspective. The questioner can seem to be implying that without some sort of a narrowly self-interested payoff, he or she is not prepared to even consider adopting the moral point of view. And many philosophers have come to think of the moral point of view as a polar alternative to the stance of selfishness. So is the questioner demanding an amoral, or even immoral, justification for morality? One Ivy League professor of philosophy once told me that he wouldn't even deign to answer anyone who asked this particular question about ethics. He seemed to have the attitude, "If you need to ask this, then don't bother to; you're morally hopeless."

But I don't think that there is anything at all wrong in principle with asking "What's in it for me?" about anything. It's a question a prudent person might ask, at least implicitly, about a lot of things.

> *Anyone informed that the universe is expanding and contracting in pulsations of eighty billion years has a right to ask, "What's in it for me?"* —PETER DE VRIES

For this is a query about self-interest, which is not the same thing as selfishness. There is nothing amoral or immoral about a healthy measure of self-interest, without which we can have no idea what it means to be interested in others. The view that ethics requires total personal disinterestedness is a dangerous distortion of the truly moral point of view. An authentically moral act or stance can serve our own interests as well as those of others.

When people ask about any proposal, idea, enterprise, or possible involvement, "What's in it for me?" they probably mean something like, "How will it affect my immediate physical safety?" or "What sort of impact will it have on my foreseeable personal comfort?" or "What will it do for my long-term financial security?" and nothing more. However, whenever we ask this sort of question about anything, we should always seek to know, "How will it affect my ultimate personal fulfillment?" Any lesser inquiry, by itself can be a bit superficial and shortsighted. When we ask the question at this deeper level about morality or ethics, a great deal of importance can be said. Doing the right thing may not always in itself protect our immediate physical safety, enhance our personal comfort, or guarantee in any obvious way our long-term financial security. But I believe that if we deeply understand what ethics is about, we can come to see that it is always connected to our long-term personal fulfillment.

The Heart of Ethics

I believe that we have lost our sense of the importance of morality because we have lost our bearings on what ethics is all about. Stephen Hawking has said that it is every physicist's dream to some day discover one law of nature that will ultimately explain absolutely everything, a law so simple that it could be printed on a T-shirt, a bumper sticker, or a business card. In philosophy, we sometimes pursue similar dreams. It would be wonderful if we could come up with a single characterization of ethics sufficient to explain what it's really all about, and yet also simple enough for a T-shirt, a bumper sticker, or a business card.

Let me give it a try. Ethics is all about:

SPIRITUALLY HEALTHY PEOPLE IN SOCIALLY HARMONIOUS RELATIONSHIPS

It may not be all that catchy, but it's true. Beneath all the philosophers' treatises about utilitarianism, deontology, and contract theory, behind all the debates over dilemmas, absolutes, and meanings, outside all the theory and metatheory, it all comes down to this: proper personal development and good dealings with others—the two sides of the moral enterprise, the inner and the outer. Spiritually healthy people in socially harmonious relationships.

I'm using the concept of spirituality here in the broadest possible sense, one that will be developed further in part four of this book. I think of the human spirit as the inner person, that aspect of each of us that differentiates us from every other form of life on this earth, however many qualities we may have in common with our nonhuman neighbors. Spiritual health is inner wholeness, stability, and strength, a state of both being and becoming in which we are realizing all that we are capable of attaining in the inner person.

Likewise, I employ the concept of harmony carefully. This ancient notion, recognized as important across very different cultures, expresses just what we are after here. Social harmony is not only a state of the absence of conflict but one of positive, vibrant consonance and interpersonal strength, a relationship within which individuals can attain the development of their highest gifts and enjoy the fullness of life together. This is the concern of ethics. The harmony of guitar strings vibrating together produces what no particular string could give rise to alone. Socially harmonious relationships among human beings can be likewise uniquely productive.

> *The harmoniousness of childhood is a gift from the hand of nature: the second harmony must spring from the labor and culture of the spirit.* —GEORG WILHELM FRIEDRICH HEGEL

Ethical Strength

So, what's in it for any of us? Nothing less, I've come to realize, than ultimate personal fulfillment. And ultimate corporate strength. Inner substance and outer greatness. Good people in good working relationships, forming together a good community out of which powerful partnerships can spring. Strength within and fulfillment together.

Too often in business today people tend to take a negative and legalistic approach to ethics as fundamentally no more than a matter of mere compliance, as if the main point of ethics or morality were just staying out of trouble, legally and otherwise. This gets the focus all wrong. Ethics is not first and foremost about staying out of trouble. It's not primarily about avoiding problems at all. Ethics is mainly about creating strength, in an individual person, a family, a community, business relationships, and life.

Anyone who thinks that the main concern of ethics is just staying out of trouble can be tempted to take a shortcut. There are typically two ways to stay out of trouble. One is to do the right thing. This can sometimes be difficult. The other path is to do whatever you want, but to camouflage it to make it look as if you're doing the right thing. One is the path of health; the other, the path of stealth. When ethics is thought of as a matter of just staying out of trouble, the path of stealth can too easily become a very strong temptation for people averse to difficulty. When it's clear that ethics is all about creating strength, the path of health is more obviously the choice to make.

Spiritually healthy people in socially harmonious relationships. Individual health and interpersonal harmony. This is the recipe for strong individuals and strong working relationships. And, of course, a noteworthy side benefit of it may very often be the avoidance of unnecessary trouble.

Ethics and Morality

I'm sure you've noticed that in talking about goodness so far, I've used "ethics" and "morality" as if they are interchangeable terms, meaning at least roughly the same thing. Some people object to this, maintaining that ethics concerns public and professional conduct, whereas morality is about private and personal values. It has even been suggested to me not only that these are different domains but that they can diverge quite a bit. I once heard a man sum it up like this: "Hey, I wear one hat at the office and another hat at home." My response was "Yes, but you wear them both on the same head." One of the great dangers we face in the modern world is an inappropriate compartmentalization of our lives.

We can draw a distinction between the public and the private, between what is professional and what is personal, but I've come to believe that the most fundamental virtues and principles in both domains are the same. In addition, I am convinced that it's dangerous to try to make exceptions to those ways of living and treating others we've found to be binding in one domain. Life is a whole, and must be approached as such.

Morals and Manners

A few years ago, I visited a beautiful school in Virginia, Hampden-Sydney College, as a guest lecturer on the topic of business ethics. My first morning there, I was walking across the campus with a very popular professor, and I noticed that every student we passed greeted us with a smile and a hearty "Good morning" or "Hello" or "How's it going?" I assumed that this was because I was in the company of this well-liked teacher. But later in the day I crossed the campus by myself, and the same thing happened. Every single student greeted me with a smile and a "Hello" or "Hi, how're you doin'?" Every single student. I've been to many friendly campuses before, but I had never seen anything quite like this.

I saw the professor later on that day and asked him about it. He answered with a big smile, "At Hampden-Sydney, we have a rule that every student must greet everyone they pass on campus." I said, "Why do you have a rule like that?" And he explained, "At Hampden-Sydney, we believe that etiquette is where ethics meets everyday life." I was quite taken by this thought and urged him to say more.

He went on, "A big part of ethics is fundamentally just other-regarding behavior. And that's precisely what etiquette is. If we don't help our students get it right in the little things, they'll never be in a position to get it right in the big things. We teach them to be courteous, hoping that this will help them to be moral."

Fascinating. And profound. When most people hear the word "ethics," or the word "morality," they often think about things like capital punishment, abortion, euthanasia, social injustice, global disarmament, insider trading, inclusiveness and harassment in the workplace, and perhaps even about legal issues such as the federal sentencing guidelines. Big issues, daunting subjects, complicated problems. But such complexities do not comprise the heart of ethics.

Ethics is not primarily about the big things; it's not the sole preserve of mind-bending dilemmas and difficult cases. It's mostly about everyday matters like how we treat the people around us and how we conduct ourselves. My friend the professor was right. If we don't get it right in the little things, we're unlikely to get it right in the big things.

> *Practice yourself, for heaven's sake, in little things; and thence proceed to greater.* —EPICTETUS

A short time after this illuminating campus visit, I received a phone call from a prominent newspaper writer. He said, "Professor Morris, this is Daniel Ruth. I'm a columnist for the *Chicago Sun-Times*, and I'm doing an article on the topic of rudeness in America." I hung up on him. No, I'm just kidding. We had a very polite and, I think, mutually enlightening conversation about an extraordinarily important issue. In many parts of America we have seen a tremendous recent increase in the level of rudeness in public places. Nearly everyone has been touched by this problem, from the simple, callous disregard of personal sensibilities to intentionally aggressive and unkind conduct. The early twentieth-century novelist Thomas Wolfe once wrote that people in cities "have no manners, no courtesy, no consideration for the rights of others and no humanity." And since his time, it's gotten much worse. Rudeness flows not only from what people say, what they do, and how they drive, but even from what's printed on their T-shirts and bumper stickers. And, of course, it's a short path from callous insensitivity to active aggression, hostility, and even violence.

If etiquette and ethics are indeed connected, then it's no surprise that we face a crisis of ethics in our time. As we'll see in the next chapter, there are many causes behind this fix. Our point here, though, is that when we talk of goodness in the workplace, and in business generally, when we talk of the moral dimension of human experience, we are not just talking about such headliner issues as sexual harassment, racial discrimination, insider trading, lying under oath, and a generally cavalier disregard of law. We're talking about basic kindness, concern, respect, caring, honor, sensitivity, and courtesy, as well as about such obviously moral issues as justice and honesty. We are talking about the conditions under which people can be their best and do their best. This is not just a matter of staying out of trouble or avoiding legal problems, but clearly involves creating strength in all our organizational and business endeavors.

Goodness in all its forms is a fundamental foundation for human excellence.

> *Goodness is true nobility.* —IPHICRATES

Liberation Ethics

When people work in conditions of perceived unfairness and unkindness, they fall into a self-protective mode. Like turtles, they crawl into their shells and hide. They're not motivated to take positive risks, to dig deep inside to discover all their talents and bring those talents to bear in creative ways on the challenges of the corporate business. Their emotions are tinged by fear and resentment, and these negative feelings block the flow of positive emotional energy they could be putting to work in their daily activities.

A group of salespeople told me that they felt they were not treated with basic kindness by the executives of their company. They were never thanked for a job well done, or praised for extraordinary accomplishment, or even greeted in the hallways. Resentment on account of these slights had risen to the extent that they admitted it was at present hard for them to do their best for the company, whereas years before, under a different management from whom they felt kindness, consideration, and positive attention in all its manifestations, their high performance seemed to flow naturally out of their daily environment.

We went on to discuss the need that existed in that particular company for the sales force to forgive management for their clear shortcomings, and in some way to teach management how to show appreciation and kindness. Some degree of leadership obviously needed to come from the front line. Until they could get over their negative feelings and help transform what had become a negative environment, they would not see the corporate results hoped for by both themselves and management. In other meetings I assisted management and top executives to recognize the existence of the problem and appreciate the importance of a solution.

Any elementary school teacher can tell you that a child who treats others badly probably comes from a home where he feels badly treated. A child who respects others most likely comes from a background where she is respected.

This is a human tendency that we usually find very difficult to outgrow. If we are treated badly in the inner circle of our lives and activities, it's hard for us to treat others well outside that circle. If there is moral goodness within, then that goodness will most likely and naturally get conveyed in turn to those outside.

In the same way, employees who feel honorably treated are most likely to pass on that honor and respect in their dealings with customers, potential customers, and vendors. Those who feel badly treated will quite often pass on some of that treatment as well to those outside the company with whom they have contact. And this can become a flash point for whether business is gained or retained. Most people find it difficult over the long run to buy even good products from bad or discourteous people.

> No one returns with good will to the place that has done him a mischief.
> —PHAEDRUS

Relationships Rule the World

In my own business endeavors, I have long had a motto: People first; projects second. If you have good relationships with people, the projects will come. And if you focus on people more than on profits, the profits generally will tend to go far beyond what you might otherwise expect. This is a fact that many businesses are beginning to see as they discern the importance of moving away from a transaction mentality and into a relationship mode.

In the course of my life so far, I have become totally loyal to any number of businesses—a gas station, a grocery store, a clothier, a travel agency, a bookstore, an automobile dealership, a restaurant—because I felt well treated in each of those places, welcomed, honored, and respected. Friendliness, kindness, genuine concern, that little extra touch, going beyond the call of duty—these are all exemplifications of basic goodness, applications of the moral dimension that often bring with them the result of loyal relationships and greater business success.

> The best portion of a good man's life,
> His little, nameless, unremembered acts
> Of kindness and of love.
> —WILLIAM WORDSWORTH

Doing Well by Doing Good

I recently moved across the country to a house at the coast with my wife, two children, and a large dog. We were driving two vehicles over a thousand miles and anticipated getting to our new house late on a Friday evening after business hours. The problem we had was that we needed a cashier's check from our new bank for the movers before they arrived very early on Saturday morning when the bank would be closed, and we couldn't even know the exact cost until after we hit the road. The new bank said they would take care of everything, and gave us a number to call after hours when we got into town. We called ahead from the interstate, and as we drove up to the recently completed house, after three days in transit, an officer of the bank was sitting in his car in our front drive, with the check we needed in his hands.

Banker extraordinaire Phil Harvell had been checking on the progress of our home for weeks as he drove by daily on his way to work. He had taken the initiative of sending us pictures of construction progress and, one week before we were to arrive, when there still wasn't any grass or landscaping in, he decided as an act of kindness not to send a last set of pictures, in hopes that things would improve before we got there. He frequently stopped and talked with the builders and brought us up to date over the phone. I should also mention that this was a man I had never met, and with whom I had no prior connections of any kind.

Three days after our arrival, Phil and his wife took us out to dinner with several friends and neighbors to help us begin to get acquainted with other people in the area. And on our first trip to the nearby branch of First Citizen's Bank, he introduced us to everyone who worked there. In the months since we moved to town, we have been uniformly treated with extraordinary friendliness and courtesy every time we enter the building. People go out of their way to help us with problems. And we always feel as if we're meeting old friends and neighbors there, never just transacting business.

It came as no surprise to me to discover that this treatment arises out of a company culture formally centered on ethical values. First Citizen's Bank has an extremely well-thought-out "Values Statement" that is intended to guide the actions of all employees. And the people there certainly do seem to create a climate of goodness, an atmosphere within which everyone can flourish. I know firsthand that it's a culture that produces customers for the long term. The people there are more important to me than the products. But I think it's also no coincidence that the products are great as well. Good people in a good environment do good work. Thoreau was right when he said that goodness is the only investment that never fails. It repays its investors in a great many ways.

The essence of business must never be viewed as the attempt to move money from other people's pockets into our own. It should be viewed as a performance art, the creation and care of structures within which people can join together in partnerships for living well.

> *Keep thyself then simple, good, pure, serious, free from affectation, a friend of justice, a worshiper of the gods, kind, affectionate, strenuous in all proper acts. Strive to continue to be such as philosophy wished to make thee. Reverence the gods and help men. Short is life.*
> —MARCUS AURELIUS

Beyond Slogans

"Doing well by doing good" has come to be one of the slogans of business ethics in the last few years. And it has many meanings. When we do something good in our communities, when we have a public presence as a force for good, public goodwill results, and goodwill often translates into good business. And this, of course, comes in many forms.

Some businesses sponsor job training programs for the community; some send their executives into the local schools to help inform and inspire students about the world of work; some spearhead charities; others volunteer to clean and paint a community center or to organize sports teams for inner-city kids. Any worthy, well-thought-out projects that reach out to the broader community can create tremendous goodwill outside the business, and can also have powerful results for a sense of pride within the business. People like to work for a company that stands for something they themselves believe in, something noble and good. Because of this, a measure of good works is never just a diversion from the main mission of a commercial enterprise but can become a solid support for that enterprise.

Nonetheless, there is a danger in thinking that "Doing well by doing good" applies only to good works outside the walls of the business, and particularly just to volunteer and charitable efforts. A main focus for doing good must always be within our own walls. Creating a climate of goodness within our businesses, within our individual and corporate endeavors, will always pay great dividends for the overall flourishing of the business.

In fact, unless the external good being done by a company is consonant with its treatment of its own employees and business partners, all such outreaches into the community will be seen by those within the company as cynical efforts to manipulate public opinion for no greater goal than positive PR and consequent financial gain. And while there is nothing at all wrong with positive PR and financial gain, employees must know that there are loftier aims behind corporate efforts in the community if they are to be genuinely inspired and ennobled by these efforts. An unethical company or amoral leadership that does "good works" for the news coverage seems so much the worse to its employees and customers who know better, precisely because of its hypocrisy. Good business must always start at home, in our treatment of our own people, in all our business dealings, and in our day-to-day decision making. What happens in the inner circle radiates outward. How this can happen will be the topic of our next two chapters.

8

The Challenge of
Ethical Action

I t's not always easy to do the right thing. There are pressures all around us that make ethical action sometimes feel like an uphill battle. In this chapter, we'll identify the most common of these pressures, get clear on the importance of truly ethical decision making, and examine the most common misconceptions about ethics in the corporate world. In doing so, we'll begin to make some exciting new discoveries about what being moral really means.

What Are the Rules Now, Anyway?

A recent book entitled *The Moral Manager*, by Clarence Walton, reported that a highly placed corporate attorney, while reflecting on the state of business ethics today, remarked, "I wonder if there are any rules now. Do people care about anything else beyond being caught? Not from where I sit."

In an article in a prominent magazine about the ethics of the stock market, written some years ago, an insider alleged that there are exactly three rules in the trade. Rule one: Never play by the rules. This, of course, is a uniquely strange rule, rendering somewhat otiose the other two, as well as itself. But we'll continue. Rule two: Never tell the truth. Rule three: Never pay in cash. A few years back, a famous deodorant commercial on TV added a fourth that would seem to fit in pretty well here: Never let them see you sweat.

> *Obtruding false rules, pranked in reason's garb.* —JOHN MILTON

What a set of rules! The game they describe is clearly one of manipulation. The driving forces seem to be greed and the lust for power. No wonder we've occasionally seen crime and chaos emerge from their domain. As a matter of fact, soon after the famous Wall Street insider trading schemes were first exposed some years ago and the high-profile players began changing their designer togs for prison couture, I was browsing through a bookstore and spotted a newly published volume with an intriguing title: *Wall Street Ethics.* I picked it up off the shelf and thumbed through it. All blank pages. Hundreds of empty pages. Nothing more. Quite a commentary.

And the bad news over the past few decades has come from all directions, not just from the New York Stock Exchange, or the savings and loan industry, or the halls of power and hotels of our nation's capital. A moral crisis seems to have enveloped all sectors of American life. If you have any doubt, take your car to a mechanic, talk to a contractor about building a house, ask around town for a lawyer you can trust, shop for a used car, or even a new car, or watch or listen to a daytime talk show. Apparently, the only guidelines for conduct widely accepted in all these contexts are:

Look out for number one.

Whatever you do, don't get caught.

And, for the more ethically sensitive and altruistic:

Mind your own business.

Of course, for the most part, this last rule applies to other people. And, interestingly, it's this third guideline that you most often hear people urging on others, in the course of which, ironically, they themselves violate it. It seems to be inbred in what passes for modern morality to be self-defeating in application as well as proclamation.

The Pressures We Face

Two executives with the largest advertising agency in the nation, disappointed with standard surveys on the beliefs and lifestyles of people in the United States, designed very carefully their own questionnaire and distributed it quite extensively, working hard to guarantee both the diversity and the anonymity of respondents. They published the surprising results in a book entitled *The Day America Told the Truth*. The news they provided on American morals is not very encouraging, and it has been confirmed by many subsequent studies. For example, 91 percent of all those surveyed reported that they tell lies on a regular basis. If this is true, then you don't really know quite what to make of all the other answers these people gave to the survey questions. And how about the answer to this question itself?

> *A liar is not believed even when he tells the truth.* —CICERO

Confusing. But I think it's safe to say that whether 91 percent of the respondents were lying or telling the truth on this particular question, we're in trouble. And, contrary to what we often hear, it's not just about trouble at the top. It's not only our leaders who lie to us, although in this one area some of them do indeed lead. The moral crisis we now face extends throughout every social stratum and touches every walk of life.

The overall picture for ethics today is challenging. It is more than a little daunting. But it need not be thought of as so bleak. We just need to get our bearings. We need to stop and think.

There are many pressures around us that make it difficult to live in a thoroughly ethical way in our business endeavors as well as in our private lives. These are forces, I believe, that are in large part responsible for many aspects of our current ethical crisis. They have subtly moved us away from a proper moral framework for our thoughts and actions. Insofar as we are subject to them, we are more likely to mistreat others, destroy our natural environment, further damage the delicate social fabric of human civilization, and in the process do tremendous unintended harm to ourselves.

Having said all that, I can't help but be reminded of Woody Allen's opening lines in his essay, "My Speech to the Graduates":

> More than any other time in history, mankind faces a crossroads. One path leads to despair and utter hopelessness. The other, to total extinction. Let us pray we have the wisdom to choose correctly.

Things are not quite that bad, though we have a lot of work ahead of us. In 1932 the Harvard philosopher Alfred North Whitehead wrote this remarkable passage:

> The behavior of the community is largely dominated by the business mind. A great society is a society in which its men of business think greatly of their functions. Low thoughts mean low behavior, and after a brief orgy of exploitation, low behavior means a descending standard of life.

This was an acutely perceptive and prophetic claim. We often use the phrase "the business world" to refer to the structures of finance, commerce, and trade, along with the array of activities directly involved in these structures. But it's a misleading phrase; it suggests a separate realm of life, a domain of existence relatively isolated from other human activities and endeavors. There is indeed a world of business. But it's a world all human beings in advanced, industrialized countries now live in, whether we are corporate executives, union members, small business owners, managers, minimum wage employees, educators, physicians, homemakers, students, or even not gainfully employed at present in any capacity. The structures of commerce affect us all.

The way people think and act in clearly business contexts filters into all other social contexts as well. Whitehead was right about the inevitable influence of business behavior on the community at large. He was right about the connection between thought and action, and he was acutely prescient about the consequences of what he called "low thoughts" and "low behavior." We are seeing many such consequences played out at the present time in corporate life, in our communities, in our nation, and in our world.

One particularly interesting feature of the pressures against ethical decision making that are prominent in corporate life is that most of them involve a narrowing of our thinking, a constricting or shrinking of the sphere of our concerns. By doing so, they render ethical decision making and ethical living more difficult, for reasons we shall see. It will be helpful to examine briefly some of the most prominent of these pervasive pressures.

Exclusively Short-Term Thinking

In most businesses, annual reports long ago gave way to quarterly reports. Monthly assessments, weekly briefings, and even daily reviews have turned up the pressure on everyone to perform in a climate of increasing immediacy. Long-term thinking has been replaced in many contexts by exclusively short-term thinking. We want results now. But in this kind of climate, the urgent easily pushes out the important.

In some manufacturing companies over the last several years, a few plant managers have actually been willing in private interviews to make extremely telling admissions. Let me give an example of one anonymous confession:

> I'm abusing my facilities. We need maintenance and repair if we're in this for the long haul. But to do that, we need some shutdown. And if I shut anything down I can't make my immediate quotas. If I produce, I get promoted out of here. So I guess I'll just have to leave the problems to the next guy.

In the meantime, what could have been small expenses become major costs. Exclusively short-term thinking can lead to destructive long-term results and create a climate in which ethical decision making is likely to be much more difficult. Some of our moral responsibilities clearly involve the long-term consequences of our actions, and in an environment of forced immediacy, these can easily be overlooked or ignored.

> *People are always much inclined to prefer present interest to the distant and remote.* —DAVID HUME

In every aspect of our lives, we're almost always in a hurry. With increasingly speedy and convenient technology of all kinds raising the pace and intensity of our days, *now* is hardly soon enough. When we think about the consequences of our actions, we tend to think only of immediate effects—quick payoffs, easy convenience. We don't look far ahead.

But of course there is a problem. I might get what I want from a certain transaction now, but how is that going to affect my prospects down the road? How is it going to affect those I do business with as time goes by? What impact will my decisions and my behavior have on the people closest to me over the long run? And what sort of person am I becoming, long-term, by the decisions I make?

Do I care about such things? I certainly should. Exclusively short-term thinking can be a very dangerous and destructive narrowing of the sphere of our concerns.

Narrow Bottom-Line Thinking

Far too easily, in many business contexts, important human values can get subordinated or simply reduced to monetary economic values, narrowly construed. All thinking becomes narrow bottom-line thinking. And, as a result, many observers have begun to suspect that Oscar Wilde's definition of *cynic* is well-applied to *business executive*: "A person who knows the price of everything and the value of nothing."

In too many businesses the only concern seems to be to make the numbers come out right. Keep the margins up. Boost the profits. Increase stock value. But what about the lives of the people who work in the business? What about their legitimate emotional needs? Their social needs? Their intellectual and professional needs? What about the community at large? What of community trust? And the natural environment? And future generations?

> *Moral principle is a looser bond than pecuniary interest.*
> —ABRAHAM LINCOLN

All such concerns and the values they reflect can easily be eclipsed by the question of money, and the other hard numbers we can easily see. The most abstract measure of property, or services, or more broadly of resources, becomes perversely the usurper of all concrete values, a focal point unto itself that crowds out all other concerns. You can't put a simple price on trust, measure easily the overall value of a particular human life, or quantify honor. It doesn't take much thought at all to see how the total dominance of narrow bottom-line thinking can clash severely with an ethical point of view. It is a further constricting of concern which, especially when combined with exclusively short-term thinking, as it most often is, can have unintentionally disastrous results.

Completely Self-Centered Thinking

The damaging consequences of myopically short-term thinking and exclusively bottom-line thinking are fairly well known and often discussed. What is not as often commented on, or even recognized, is another kind of pressure, which creates another extremely dangerous narrowing of concern. Many business people over the last several decades have experienced what some psychologists call "mobility panic." They have been transferred from one town to another, from one part of the country to another, over and over. To advance to greater challenges or higher pay, they've had to relocate on a fairly regular basis. Look down almost any street in desirable suburban middle management and executive neighborhoods, and you'll see a For Sale sign or even a moving van on the job.

One friend of mine, just out of college and working for a major manufacturing company, lived in thirteen different cities over a period of thirteen months. It sounded like such an adventurous lifestyle—living in great cities like San Francisco, Charlotte, Boston, and Salt Lake City, and an affiliation with a big-name company—but when I really talked with him about it, he confessed that all he ever got to see was his apartment or the manufacturing facility or sales center in each locale. Only by phoning friends at night did he hear all the great features of whatever city he happened to be in. He was up early for work, strapped in the car for a long commute, working too many hours getting to know the business in each new facility, and then returning to his apartment too late and too tired for anything like a night on the town. He never got to know his neighbors, many of whom were nearly as mobile, and never had a chance to learn much about the community.

This is certainly an extreme case, but the general phenomenon is disturbingly pervasive. When people move frequently, it's difficult for them to establish any real identity in a community. Not surprisingly, their concerns and loyalties narrow from the community as a whole to just the business itself. The corporation offers the only source of identity. It becomes the only community the manager or executive knows well. And so, very soon, the business becomes more important than any larger civic community sustaining it.

Of course, many businesses themselves these days have become very unstable environments. There are hostile takeovers, mergers, and restructurings of every kind, resulting in layoffs and downsizings as a threat at nearly every level. In such an environment, a man or woman's own career can easily seem vastly more important than the business itself, and more important than relationships with any group of people at work. This is nothing more than a further shrinking of the sphere of personal concern, one which can lead directly to completely self-centered thinking.

The popular contemporary writer Tom Wolfe said years ago that in his research on one book project, he had occasion to interview the heads of many major American corporations. He claims he was very surprised and quite disillusioned to discover how little loyalty there seemed to be at the top. Many executives expend great energy and ingenuity providing for their own compensation packages and "golden parachutes," should things go sour or the business go down, eventualities made more likely by their own self-directed focus of attention and effort. In too many businesses, facilities have decayed and employees have suffered as top executive compensation packages shoot through the stratosphere.

> *Man seeks his own good at the whole world's cost.*
>
> —ROBERT BROWNING

How does all this affect personal decision making? We all know the answer to this one. When loyalty to the business has eclipsed loyalty to the community, the impact of a decision on the community may hardly even be considered. It won't be *understood.* And when there is little or no loyalty to the company itself, all that really counts is figuring out, in the narrowest possible sense, "What's in it for me?"

The problem is usually intensified by the fact that when this question dominates a person's thinking, it's often asked only within fairly short-term or bottom-line horizons of further narrowness. What we get is exactly what we see around us in the world today, the lifestyles of the rich and famous hovering above the debris of a culture in trouble. In fact, the well-known TV program could easily have done a great many of its segments over the past couple of decades on the grounds of minimum-security federal prisons. That's where completely self-centered thinking in positions of power too often has led.

The Cult of Personality

Self-centered thinking is reinforced and encouraged throughout our society by a kindred force dominating much of our cultural life, the cult of personality. We're exposed to so many images of the great successful individual surrounded by all of his or her possessions. We have numerous television shows that profile these titans and their toys, as well as newspapers and magazines that report their every exploit and weave myths around their glamorous lives. In the business world we hear of great icons of success like Bill Gates, Donald Trump, and Ted Turner. In the music world, there have long been such towering figures as Frank Sinatra, Elvis Presley, Michael Jackson, and Madonna. In basketball there is, of course, Michael Jordan, and many lesser lights of notoriety and accomplishment. In every sport, as well as in the movies, the "name" players command the money and fame that capture the dreams of the average person.

This focus on the single successful individual in any field of endeavor, this cult of personality, is often encouraged by some of the stars themselves every bit as much as by their PR people. One such individual's first book, an account of his own life, was a big national best-seller. Approached by his publisher to consider putting his name to another book, he is said to have replied, "I can't think of another interesting topic."

In our cultural fixation on these individual giants of fortune, we easily forget about all the other people always behind the scenes, and the relationships that have made their success possible. With this narrow conception of accomplishment and consequent fixation on individual personalities, we're then easily tempted to focus on cultivating our own "personalities"—our charm, wit, and gregariousness, or a commanding bearing and briskness of speech, or even an eccentric "creative genius" persona—to the neglect of building our character. We concentrate on designing a "look" to present to the world, to get the sort of attention that will include us in that gallery of dominating personalities ourselves, whether on a local or national level. And if we succeed, we have created appearance to the neglect of moral reality, in pursuit of what is itself nothing more than an illusion.

Going with the Flow

We're all familiar with the term *peer pressure*. How many times have we felt a pressure to conform when we've heard people say things like, "Hey, we're all in this thing together," "Don't rock the boat," "We need you to be a team player," "This is the way we do things around here," or "Sometimes you've just got to go with the flow"? In every group there is pressure to conform, whether or not it's ever expressed in words. Have you ever said to yourself, about something you're otherwise unsure of, and perhaps very uncomfortable with, "Well, it looks like everyone's doing it that way. Maybe that's just how things are done around here"?

If there isn't ethical behavior in a group you're thrown in with, there will be a strong pressure on you to behave in the same way. If your workplace is a setting where people cut corners, stretch the truth, and act from obvious considerations of mere expediency (and these are, of course, all well-known euphemisms for unethical conduct), and if those around you tend to forget the genuinely human element in dealing with others, the pressure will be on you to do the same. It's hard to swim against the current, especially over a long period. This is why it's in our own interest to do everything within our power to minimize our association with the wrong kind of people, as many of the great thinkers have advised.

> *Associate not with evil men, lest you increase their number.*
> —GEORGE HERBERT

The pressure to be a team player can of course be a good thing or a bad thing, depending on the team. If things are done well, with excellence and within a firm ethical framework, this can be a great spur to personal growth, a motivation or incentive for improvement, a real force for good. But in the wrong environment, this pressure can have tremendously detrimental effects. Conformity can sometimes have its rewards. But we must not forget to count its costs.

The Bored and the Restless

Another pressure in ethical decision making we commonly face is especially applicable to the young, but it is no respecter of age. It is the pressure of a void. As the early natural philosophers used to say, "Nature abhors a vacuum." Especially when the void or vacuum is the utter emptiness of boredom.

In a recent study of unethical behavior, a surprising number of people who were interviewed admitted that they often found themselves tempted to break the rules, or to step outside the bounds of morally proper conduct, simply because of the need for a little excitement. Life, they said, is too often boring. Every now and then, we need to inject some raisins of excitement into the otherwise dull dough of existence. We need to shake a little hot sauce into the soup of the day and spice it up. This is, of course, a classic example of the age-old lure of forbidden fruit, the emotional rush of trying to get away with something prohibited.

The twentieth-century British philosopher Bertrand Russell wrote, "Boredom is . . . a vital consideration for the moralist, since at least half the sins of mankind are caused by the fear of it." In our complex, fascinating, and fast-moving world, what can possibly be the source of all this boredom? The French existentialist philosopher Jean-Paul Sartre, one of the group of early twentieth-century thinkers most concerned with the deepest paradoxes of human existence in the world, wondered about this subject. "What is boredom?" he wrote. "It is when there is simultaneously *too much* and *not enough*." A lot is packed into this simple and very wise statement.

> *Repose is a good thing, but boredom is its brother.* —VOLTAIRE

Boredom occurs when there is simultaneously too much and not enough—at work, it can sometimes be a combination of too much comfort and not enough challenge, or too much of the same and not enough of the new, too much repetition and not enough creation. In society at large, it's often a combination of too much privilege with not enough responsibility, too much on the outside with not enough on the inside, too much to enjoy with not enough to work toward, or even too much to view with not enough to value.

Anyone who is not learning and growing and feeling an intrinsic value in what they are doing is vulnerable to the eventual encroachment of this condition. But if we have good work, if it serves a higher purpose and involves creative engagement, learning, and the building of fulfilling relationships, boredom is much less likely to undermine ethical decision making and ethical action.

The Ethical and the Nonethical

It may be helpful at this point to offer a brief preliminary characterization of some differences between an ethical and a nonethical point of view, as well as between the ethical and the nonethical person. These are rough-and-ready contrasts, but they will help us get a proper perspective on the nature and importance of ethical decision making in our lives. They will also help to provide a perspective on what it takes to resist the pressures we've identified.

The nonethical point of view is, typically, narrow and shortsighted. The ethical point of view is, by contrast, broad and long-range. This is not to say that a selfish, immoral egoist can't engage in broad, long-range planning. But the length and breadth of his planning will take place only within the self-imposed narrow confines of his own perceived self-interest. The ethical person, on the other hand, will consider the strengths of long-range planning as compared with the promised immediacies of short-term personal gain.

Truly long-range thinking must of necessity transcend the concerns of the self at the present time. The short term is the more typical range of the unethical go-getter. I believe it is our increasing inability to engage in short-term sacrifice for the sake of long-term gain, as well as our inability to engage in self-sacrifice for the sake of any broader social gain, that is behind so many of our current cultural problems.

The unethical person has an exclusive allegiance, either to self or to something that has captured the self—a cause, a cult, a charismatic individual, or a favored group of people. The ethical person has a much more inclusive concern.

When you stop to think about it, the difference between exclusivity and inclusivity is tremendously important. Exclusivity of concern, value, or allegiance is the source of so much of the strife, hatred, distrust, and injustice in our world. Me against you, my family against your family, my social group against yours, my racial group against another, my department against other departments, my company against yours, my country against the world. Exclusivity of concern is a prescription for social disaster.

The history of human ethical enlightenment is the history of increasing inclusivity. We have reason to believe that early in human history, moral obligations and relations were thought to hold only within the family or within a tribe of families. Anyone outside the tribe, a stranger, was a threat and an enemy or, worse yet, a "nonperson," not even recognized as having any status in the distinctively moral realm at all. Human moral awakening has consisted in part in extending that sphere of concern across artificial boundaries, as well as beyond natural boundaries.

The greatest challenge we face nowadays in our intricately interconnected world society is to be truly universal in our ethical concerns. And ethical tribalism, in various manifestations, is one of the greatest dangers in corporate life today. Whenever goodness is established within an inner circle, it must then serve as a foundation for building outward, extending that goodness as far as possible throughout all the relationships in which we stand.

> *Morality, when vigorously alive, sees farther than intellect.*
>
> —J. A. FROUDE

Ethical Decision Making

Let's take just a moment to look at the basic structure of decision making. Some people think it's a very simple thing: You have a problem, you make a decision. And that's all there is to it.

Problem >> Decision

But it's certainly not that simple.

First, we need to be aware that what we see our problems as is always a result of the beliefs and values through which we look at life, as if through a lens. Two people can confront the same situation and yet think of themselves as facing two very different problems. The way we represent the structure of decision making should take this into account.

> *If decisions were a choice between alternatives, decisions would come easy. Decision is the selection and formulation of alternatives.*
>
> —KENNETH BURKE

In addition, we typically don't simply see a problem through the lens of our beliefs and values and then decide to solve it. In any difficult situation, we may first consider a range of possible solutions, decide on a subset of these as feasible plans we could live with, and finally opt to put one of them into action. This is more like a two-level decision-making process. So, then, given any objective decision-making situation, we have:

Beliefs + Values	>>	Perceived Problem	>>	Decision #1 Feasible Options We Could Take	>>	Decision #2 Option to Put into Action

But even this leaves out an important fact about the logic of decision making.

Where do our problems come from? Of course, they come from a variety of directions, but one thing that's easily forgotten is that we always have our present problems to some extent because of our past decisions. I was once a rock guitarist. If I had chosen to stay in the music business, I would have very different problems to solve today from those I have as a philosopher. And you can say something similar about yourself. If you had gone to a different school, had majored in something else, or just had taken a different job, you most likely would be faced with very different problems from those you confront at present. Now of course certain types of problems are universal, so that no matter what you do, you'll have to face them. But the form in which they come to you will differ depending on choices you have made, and many problems will come to you only because of the decisions you've made and the actions you've taken in the past.

Prior Decisions >> Present Problems

The author Robert Fulghum tells a great story about the volunteers of a small-town fire department who had to rush to a house where smoke was billowing from an upstairs window. They broke down the door and, climbing the stairs, found a man in a burning bed. Pulling him off the flaming mattress, they secured his safety and then asked him how the fire in the bed had started. His reported answer gave Fulghum the title for his second best-selling book. The man said "I don't know. It was on fire when I lay down on it."

Poor decision-making skills were clearly in evidence here. Few of us are challenged by decision-making difficulties at quite this level, but the story does make a good general point. Just like this poor man, we all sometimes have to be rescued from the consequences of our decisions. Our present problems are always to some extent the result of our previous decisions. And with this in mind, it becomes clear how important it is to make good decisions.

> *It is always thus, impelled by a state of mind which is destined not to last, that we make our most irrevocable decisions.*
>
> —MARCEL PROUST

Philosophers throughout history have grappled with the question of how we can most reliably make good decisions. And there are basically only two distinct answers to the question. The first, we will explore in the rest of this chapter. The other will be the subject of our next chapter.

Playing by the Rules

A great number of philosophers seem to have agreed for a very long time that for good ethical decision making, we need rules, lots and lots of rules. This comes from a moral perspective that holds that the realm of ethics is comprised wholly of rules for living, for behavior within a given profession, and for life generally—rules for lawyers, rules for real estate brokers, rules for members of financial institutions, rules for human beings in relationships with others. In this view, goodness is a matter of following the rules. And unethical conduct, then, is seen as breaking a rule, or a group of rules.

In this approach to ethics, the emphasis is on compliance: Don't falsify reports. Don't steal from the company. Don't betray the confidence of a client. Don't make false promises. Don't cheat a customer. Don't violate the regulatory laws governing your industry. Before you act, check the rules. Or ask a lawyer. Ethics is defined as playing by the rules, and any company concerned with ethics has to do two things: It has to promulgate clear statements of what the rules are, and it has to devise checking procedures to see to it that everyone is playing by those rules. Many companies compile ethics handbooks for their employees and appoint ethics or compliance officers to oversee the conduct of everyone within the company.

I have one friend who, some years ago, gave a number of ethics seminars to major companies. He tells me that he often asked executives if they were in the process of compiling any sort of book of ethical rules for the workforce. If they said yes, he asked them, to their considerable surprise, to please stop.

His reasoning was that books of rules almost never help. The bad people will find loopholes and other ways around the rules, and the good people, who would do the right thing anyway, waste a lot of their time and energy checking what exactly the rules require before they act—"Wait a minute, I've got to be sure this complies with Rule 37, Part B, Clauses 1–3a"—and then maybe action is too late.

> *The more laws, the less justice.* —GERMAN PROVERB

Michael Josephson, Founder of the Josephson Institute for the Advancement of Ethics, told Bill Moyers in a PBS television interview that he once taught ethics in a law school with this legalistic approach: Here are the rules, and here's how to use them for your convenience and profit. Then his first child was born. He says that, after reflecting on his son's future, he asked himself the question: "Do I want my son to grow up in a world where people think about ethics the way I teach the subject?" And he realized that the answer was no. So he stopped teaching the rule approach to ethics. He stopped teaching ethics to lawyers at all. He resigned his position in the law school and founded an institute for the study of ethics, seeking to ascertain more deeply what ethics really are.

It's natural for us to propound rules for almost anything that we do, and then to think of them as being of the first importance. They seem to eliminate some of the uncertainties from life. For example, I took a short break from writing today and went with my children to our neighborhood swimming pool. As I sat at the edge of the water for a moment of philosophical reflection, I overheard Matt and Sara discussing animatedly a game of pool tag they wanted to play with each other. After listening a few minutes, I had to smile as I realized that they were just standing there in waist-deep water, spending so much time on making up, negotiating, and refining the rules they would adhere to that they would have very little time left for actually playing the game. What a foreshadowing of and metaphor for so much adult life! Rules can be very important, but there are things that are even more important. Ethics must go beyond the mere formulation and monitoring of rules. We have a game to play as well, and we need to get on with it.

It's Not Just Rules

When most people in business think of ethics nowadays, they seem to think of nothing more than rules. But there are some major problems with the conception of ethics as having to do with nothing more than lots of rules. Let me briefly mention just a few.

First of all, there can never be enough specific rules to cover everything we recognize as an ethical situation. Life is far too complex. The rules could never be complete.

Second, because of this complexity of real life, the promulgation of rules as the entirety of the ethical dimension of life can encourage an "exception," or loophole mentality, a manipulative mindset that ends up being anything but ethical.

> *There is no rule without an exception.* —CERVANTES

Third, rules can conflict. If ethics is nothing but following rules and two rules conflict, requiring of us different and incompatible actions, how do we find a solution? Do we need rules to tell us how to adjudicate conflicts among the rules? And what about these further rules themselves?

Fourth, a related problem is that all rules need interpretation. If ethics were just a matter of rules, we'd need rules for the interpretation of the rules. But then, these would need interpreting also, and so on, and on and on. If ethics were nothing but rules, we'd need infinitely many rules, and that's absurd. So there has to be more to ethics than just lots of rules and a concern for applying those rules.

> *Rules and precepts are of no value without natural capacity.*
> —QUINTILIAN

Don't misunderstand me. There is nothing wrong with having ethical or moral rules. And I personally have no problem with succinct books of rules in business life if they are appropriately used and put into the proper context. Rules serve a number of functions. In early character development, rules can point a child in a proper direction. We give our young children lots of rules, and as they mature, fewer are necessary, if all goes well. Rules can also serve to create mutually assured sets of expectations in a profession or in a business. At some level, we can't do without at least basic rules.

A friend of mine does business around the world. Before his first trip to Italy, he had been told that Italians don't operate by any rules at all. He had heard that the place is total chaos. But he witnessed something amazing during his first hour there, in his ride from the airport. He swears this is true. The Italian businessman who picked him up after his international flight seated him in a sports car and took off. They sped down twisty roads and approached an intersection with no apparent cross traffic, but their light was clearly red. The guy didn't even slow down. Zoom, right through the stoplight. They then came to a second intersection. Another red light. The driver slowed a little, but proceeded on through at a fairly breezy clip. Finally, at a third intersection, where shrubs and trees blocked any view of cross traffic, the light was green. The driver screeched to a stop. My astonished friend, who up until then had been nervously silent on the topic of their drive together, finally spoke up. He said, "What's going on? You just ran two red lights, and now you get a green and you stop?" The Italian just looked over and said, "I gotta stop. Cross traffic has red, and some guy might be coming through."

Rules. Even the Italians, who sometimes may seem not to have them, have them. We really can't do without them. But in the end, we also need something more than rules.

The Greatest Rule of All

Rules can serve to articulate at least the main parameters of what is expected of everyone. They can coordinate human behavior in at least a rough and ready way. They can also convey part of a company's corporate culture in a very simple form. They lay down a grid for acceptable behavior. They delineate the sorts of things that are done and the things that are not to be done.

And some simple moral rules can serve to summarize large tracts of human experience, as well as to remind us of our moral bearings in difficult situations. Let me give you the most important example of what I mean.

There is one rule recognized in some form or other within every major human culture I have been able to investigate. And increasingly, corporate leaders today are beginning to testify to its fundamental value in their business endeavors. Its evident power intimates some of the potential usefulness of moral rules in general, despite any difficulties we might have in conceiving of ethics as involving nothing but rules. This rule can be identified quite dramatically by the briefest of ancient anecdotes.

History tells us that the great Jewish scholar Hillel (c. 30 B.C.–A.D. 10) was once asked what, at its essence, Judaism really is, and replied simply: "Don't do to others what you wouldn't want done to you. All the rest is commentary." What a statement! The most eminent scholar of the intricacies of Judaic law, with all the immense detail of its prescriptions, as well as the whole sweep of its history, views it all as mere commentary on something like what we have come to know in another formulation as the Golden Rule: Do unto others as you would have them do unto you. Treat others the way you would want to be treated in their place.

This is probably the most famous moral rule ever promulgated. And it's found in culture after culture, in every time and place. It's expressed in many different forms, but the main thrust is remarkably the same. Here are a few examples.

Confucianism:	"Do not do unto others what you would not want them to do unto you."
Buddhism:	"Seek for others the happiness you desire for yourself. Hurt not others with that which pains you."

Hinduism:	"All your duties are included in this: Do nothing to others that would pain you if it were done to you."
Judaism:	"That which is hurtful to you, do not do to your fellow man."
Islam:	"Let none of you treat his brother in a way he himself would not like to be treated. No one of you is a believer until he loves for his brother what he loves for himself."
Taoism:	"View your neighbor's gain as your own gain, and your neighbor's loss as your own loss."
Christianity:	"Do unto others as you would have them do unto you."

Notice that the Golden Rule, in its positive formulation, does not say:

Do unto others as they do unto you.

This is known as the Rule of Reciprocity. It counsels you to allow others to call the shots for you. They act, you react. When you live by this rule, you give up your own integrity and merely respond, chameleon-like, to how others are treating you. We'll have more to say about this later.

Also, the Golden Rule does not say:

Do unto others before they do unto you,

which I call the First Strike Principle. It's a motto of aggressive gamesmanship and has guided far too much conduct in the world of business in the past twenty years.

Finally, the Golden Rule doesn't say:

Do unto others as they would be done unto,

or "Treat others the way they want to be treated." I call this permutation, sometimes confused with the Golden Rule, the General Obedience Rule. What if someone wants to be treated in an unfairly preferential way? Should a central moral rule direct you to indulge them in this unethical desire? And if someone perversely wanted to be treated badly, no moral principle should oblige you to comply. But there is something deeper to be noted here as well.

The Golden Rule, as it is stated properly, appeals to our imaginations. It tells me to treat another person the way I would want to be treated if I were in his position. I can't be guided by it without imagining what it would feel like to be in that other person's situation, with all her morally legitimate concerns and desires. The Golden Rule directs me to use my imagination in such a way as to create empathy for others. I believe that the imagination is the single greatest natural power in human life. And so I think it's no coincidence that the greatest moral rule appeals to exactly that power.

An imaginatively empathetic application of the Golden Rule can yield tremendous results in any organization. The legendary creator of the Visa card and organizational innovator Dee Hock could even present this as his "Ph.D. in Leadership, Short Course":

> Make a careful list of all things done to you that you abhorred. Don't do them to others, ever. Make another list of things done for you that you loved. Do them for others, always.

Understanding and Using the Golden Rule

Some people worry about the role of the Golden Rule in business. At a panel discussion on business ethics once held at Notre Dame, Leo Lindbeck, one of the world's greatest builders, from Houston, Texas, spoke inspiringly about this rule of conduct. A young man in the back of the room raised his hand. When called on, he said, "Mr. Lindbeck, I'm in the building industry too, but I've been in it for only three years. What you said just now in praise of the Golden Rule was very moving, but I've got a problem. My job is negotiating. What happens if I go into a room to negotiate a deal and I feel bound to treat the other guy in accordance with the Golden Rule, but he feels no such ethical constraints on his conduct? Won't that put me at a significant tactical disadvantage, in effect tying my hands behind my back? Won't the guy who's not bound by ethical or moral constraints be more likely to win the day?"

> *Behold, I send you forth as sheep in the midst of wolves: be ye therefore wise as serpents and harmless as doves.* —JESUS OF NAZARETH

Lindbeck considered for a moment and gave a great reply. He said, "If the first time that you ever see this guy you're going to be negotiating with is when you walk into that room to cut the deal, then you're a fool. To be an ethical businessman, you've got to be shrewd. You've got to plan ahead. 'Ethical' is not the same thing as 'naive.' Get to know the other guy you'll be negotiating with as far in advance as possible, weeks or even months ahead of time if you can. Get to know him as a person. Let him get to know you. In every little way, in each of your contacts with him, treat him in accordance with the Golden Rule. Most people mirror back the treatment they receive. The more you treat him with respect and concern, the more difficult you'll make it for him to do otherwise to you. And then, when you do go in to negotiate the deal, if he still treats you in a morally dubious way, walk away from it. You can't make a good deal with a bad person."

Shrewd. Brilliant. And right. Ethical business is the best kind of business. The Golden Rule can be the best possible guide to morally strong and sustainable business relations if it's applied properly.

> *Goodness is easier to recognize than to define.* —W. H. AUDEN

All rules need interpretation, and in the final analysis, moral interpretation must come from somewhere beyond the realm of rules. We need to be able to see behind the rules to the underlying realities. But what moral territory is there beyond or behind the realm of rules? Is there some other source of ethical guidance besides explicit principles and formulated regulations? Is there something other than rules that could help us to make good ethical decisions? An important, recently rediscovered tradition of moral reflection says yes. And that is precisely the topic of our next chapter.

9

Wisdom, Virtue, and Corporate Strength

I n answer to the question, "How do we make good, ethical decisions?" the previous chapter explored the traditional suggestion that we need lots of rules to govern our decision making. But rules must be rooted in something deeper if they are to bear proper fruit in our lives. Companies and organizations that are rule-focused and compliance-driven see only part of the picture. But we can't benefit from the strongest, most positive corporate spirit unless we nurture it with a more fundamental insight about ethics. And that's what we'll explore together in this chapter.

Fertile Soil for Growing Good Business

How do we make good decisions? How do we conduct ourselves properly in the most ethical way? The answer derives from Aristotle: We need wisdom and virtue in our lives.

Wisdom and virtue. Two old-fashioned words just recently returning to fashion. The modern workplace cannot function well over the long run without the benefit of wisdom and virtue. Good decisions can't be made in challenging times without these qualities. People can't be their best or do their best without relying on both the wisdom to see what ought to be done and the virtue required for doing it. But if this is so, then we need to ask, what exactly are these ancient attributes of wisdom and virtue?

> *Wisdom is a solid and entire building, of which every piece keeps its place and bears its mark.* —MICHEL EYQUEM DE MONTAIGNE

We'll start with a few quick definitions. Wisdom is just deep insight about living. Good advice from the realm of experience. A keen perception of what is right. Virtue is the habit or disposition of acting in accordance with wisdom. Doing the wise thing. Simple to say, but sometimes hard to manage.

In ancient Latin, *virtu* meant "strength." In even more ancient Greek, there was a word, *arete*, that meant both "ethics" and "excellence," and that could also be understood as conveying a notion of strength. Virtue should be seen as that deep wellspring of ethical tendency that joins with wisdom to create in us the most important form of human strength, the strength of moral character, or integrity, the sort of strength that leads to long-term human excellence. This strength is always a result of what human beings are like as people. It's always a consequence of character.

We often speak of "character" and "integrity," but many people would find it difficult to say exactly what these things are. Philosophically, however, they are easy to define. I have come to believe that a person's character is his or her settled degree of wisdom and virtue, an established pattern of thought, feeling, and behavior that has arisen out of repeated action and reaction in the world. Character is then the sum total of all those morally relevant habits that we have developed. It is also the source of our most immediate, as well as our most reflective, responses to the world.

> *Our characters are the result of our conduct.* —ARISTOTLE

Integrity is a function of character. Etymologically, consider for a moment the words *integer*, "whole number," and *integration*, "the bringing together of disparate parts into one whole." Likewise, we can see the meaning of *integrity* most clearly as having to do with oneness and wholeness. You deal with a situation with integrity when you bring the wholeness of who you are, what you believe in, and what you most deeply value to that situation, and when your beliefs and values are positively connected to what is true and what is good. Integrity does not let you deviate from the wholeness of your values for the sake of temporary gain with respect to one of those values. It does not allow you to disregard the demands of truth and goodness in deciding what you will do. The measure of a person's integrity can be thought of as the result of her general level of wisdom and virtue together.

In an individual, integrity is a sign of good character. In an organization, integrity is a sign of good culture. These are the two poles around which all of business ethics spins: individual character and institutional culture. If you have the right people around you, and all of you have good conditions in which to work, you see the results of both character and culture linked in a positive way. On an individual level, a bad character, and on an institutional level, a bad culture, equally have self-destructive results.

Unethical Means Self-Destructive

Unethical practices are always self-destructive over the long run, on both a personal and an organizational level. A famous duel in American history can serve as a good metaphor for this truth. Alexander Hamilton had been George Washington's secretary of the treasury, and was founder of the Bank of New York and the Bank of the United States. Aaron Burr had been vice president under Thomas Jefferson, and had broken Hamilton's banking monopoly by founding what is now Chase Manhattan Bank. Hamilton, who apparently viewed Burr as an unwelcome rival, placed a spy among his stockholders and even had his brother-in-law, John Church, who was a professional dueler, insult Burr publicly in such a way as to provoke a duel. Burr emerged unscathed, aside from having a button shot off his vest. But some time later, Hamilton himself reportedly issued a scathing and public insult to provoke a second duel, in preparation for which he borrowed a set of trick pistols from Church, planning an unfair advantage over Burr. Each pistol in the pair had a secret hair trigger, called now a single-set trigger. By pushing his slightly forward, Hamilton would be able to position it in such a way as to fire much more easily and quickly than Burr, who would not know of this feature of the guns and so would be at a severe, and unfair, disadvantage. The guns also had weighted forestocks and a larger bore than usual, features which also would have disqualified them as dueling pistols. We have to remember that, strange as it now seems, dueling was then an honor-bound tradition governed by strict rules and conventions. Hamilton apparently wanted a duel but without the rules.

The duel took place, and Hamilton was brought down by his own tricks. His gun, set to require only a half pound of pull, fired far too easily, up into the air before he could even point it at his opponent, and Burr, working with the normal ten to twelve pounds of pull on his trigger, was able to take careful aim and, unintentionally aided by the other illicit features of the gun chosen by his adversary, hit Hamilton dead on, the overly large .54 caliber ball lodging in his liver and killing him within thirty-six hours.

> *Evil on itself shall back recoil.* —JOHN MILTON
>
> • • •
>
> *His own crime besets every man.* —CICERO

Putting aside for a moment the ethical status of dueling itself, the approach used by Hamilton within this practice captures vividly in metaphorical fashion the self-defeating nature of unethical action. Hoist by his own petard, undone by his own doing, the unethical person cuts off the branch on which he himself is sitting.

In summarizing what can be learned from studying nonhuman life on earth, a prominent biologist recently told the *New York Times* that two lessons stand out. One is that in most circumstances of challenge and adaptation, small is better than big. This, of course, is a lesson that has been learned in many businesses in recent years as we have witnessed the need to break large organizations into much smaller groups and teams.

The second lesson from the world of biology is that although predators succeed over the short run, cooperators win in the end. Translated more broadly, this might be interpreted as a warning about unethical power plays and sharp practices. Can an unethical person have success? Certainly, a bad person can have sometimes outrageous levels of success. For a while. In a limited domain. And at the expense of what really matters. But in the long run, an unethical approach will never produce lasting good.

What Goes Around Comes Around

> *It always surprises me that otherwise intelligent people don't realize that if you treat people badly, it will eventually come back to you.*
>
> —CHARLES GRODIN

In the previous chapter, during our discussion of the famous Golden Rule, I mentioned what is often called *The Rule of Reciprocity*, the principle of doing unto others as they do unto us. As a matter of somewhat lamentable fact, most of us easily lapse into this mode of reactive conduct in our business dealings and private lives. If someone treats us well, we mirror back that conduct and treat them well. But if they treat us badly, then they'd better watch out. And of course it's not hard to turn this around. If we treat someone else well, they are likely to respond in kind. But if we treat them badly, we'll eventually reap what we have sowed.

> *I do unto others what they do unto me, only worse.* —JIMMY HOFFA
>
> • • •
>
> *If you start throwing hedgehogs under me I shall throw two porcupines under you.* —NIKITA KHRUSHCHEV

As the great first century philosopher Seneca once said, you must expect to be treated by others as you have treated them or, he could have added, worse. The lesson of this is clear. Using the Golden Rule as much as we can is the only possible way to create for ourselves the sort of interpersonal environment it can be deeply enjoyable to experience.

An unethical individual can mistreat people, and cheat and betray customers, colleagues, and suppliers fairly easily one at a time. But after a while, because of the natural prevalence of reciprocity in human behavior, he will end up with an adversarial army out there prepared to do likewise or worse to him and bring him down hard. This is one of the reasons unethical practices are self-defeating in the long run.

> *And those who have been wronged, or believe themselves to be wronged, are terrible; for they are always looking out for their opportunity.* —ARISTOTLE

Another mechanism for the self-destruction of unethical practices is even simpler. When associates see their colleagues, supervisors, managers, or executives treat people outside the company in unethical ways, they naturally become wary of how they themselves will be treated in the future by these people in their own organization. A person capable of treating anyone unethically is capable of treating everyone unethically. We naturally recoil at some level from people who treat others manipulatively, knowing that we ourselves could easily receive that same treatment if it came to be perceived as expedient.

This is a subtle but important point. Companies that advertise their products with outrageously artificially faked up photographs ("enhanced imagery") and market them with groundless hyperbole also in most cases unintentionally erode internal confidence that inter-office communications from the top are anything more than similarly manipulative hype. Perhaps even worse, companies or executives who take public stances of an ethical nature that are out of step with their internal policies or practices just for the sake of the PR value to be derived encourage mistrust and cynicism within the workforce. People naturally feel that if the executives are hosing down the public, then they're probably doing the same to their employees.

Human beings are naturally cautious and on guard about being misled. This is a straightforward adaptive trait with clear survival value. And it's tied to our deep need for truth. The wariness and mistrust generated by corporate hypocrisy of any kind is an acid completely destructive of positive corporate spirit. Over the long run, any behavior that generates this response, however beneficial it might have seemed in the short term, is ultimately self-destructive.

> *I hate the man who is double-minded, kind in words but a foe in his conduct.* —PALLADAS

Consequences of Corruption

The self-defeating nature of unethical practices becomes clear in many different ways. Consider for a moment the involvement of large corporations in our political process. Many recent editorial commentators have bemoaned the influence of major corporations on the political processes of the United States. But of course there's no turning back. With the unprecedented importance of these large, nonsovereign human organizations, there is no getting the genie back into the bottle. And I'm not convinced that we should want to. Large companies are tremendous pools of well-organized talent with impressive information gathering and disseminating capacities. To exclude such resources from the political process, even if it were possible, would probably be very foolish. And yet much of modern corporate political involvement has not been entirely salutary, to put it extremely mildly.

So much recent lobbying activity has been driven by exclusively short-term, bottom-line, narrowly self-interested mentality that the results for the nation as a whole have often been destructive. Corporate influence is not in itself a bad thing at all. It is only unethical and narrowly self-interested influence that is problematic. If companies could be taught to act in their own enlightened, long-term interests and shown how this is tied up with the long-term well-being of other interest groups, as well as of the overall society, their efforts could enhance, and not erode, the general effectiveness of the political process. As it is, unethical practices and policies have generated a significant public backlash, making it more difficult, in unanticipated ways, for those corporations themselves to flourish, as well as for their employees to live well and happily. This is one way in which inappropriate political action can have self-defeating consequences.

It is well known that individuals in roles of public trust sometimes yield to inappropriate influence in betrayal of their responsibilities, rationalize to themselves the whole process, and finally end up getting rewarded by high-paying jobs in those companies their decisions have helped, once their government tenure ends. This revolving door is problematic in a variety of ways. For one thing, the corrupting company hires a corrupted and therefore provably corruptible person into an executive position, a person whose true character, or lack thereof, is most often hidden from his own self-understanding behind a veneer of rationalization and self-deception. As we'll discuss further in just a bit, people tend to become like the people they are around. The presence of another corrupt individual in an already corrupt company can only push the process of unethical degradation further along. The individual is likely to become worse in his new circumstances, reaping the supposed rewards of his past wrongdoing and thus sinking further into the cloud of ethical blindness. And another thing happens. The company that helped corrupt him becomes even worse due to the presence in its midst of one more corrupt person.

> *Trust not to rotten planks.*
>
> —WILLIAM SHAKESPEARE, *ANTONY AND CLEOPATRA*

This latter point is true for more than in-principle reasons. A person corrupted by one source can be corrupted by another. How can his new associates trust a man who has once already sold out his character to the highest bidder? How can a woman who has betrayed previous colleagues and responsibilities enter into a fully collaborative partnership with the people who have already manipulated her for their own interests, and she them for hers? Is there any honor among thieves? It's easy to see how unethical practices produce dynamically unstable relationships and results not guaranteed to work for the greatest good of the greatest number, or for any real long lasting good at all.

I don't want to sound unduly shrill about all this, but it is important to make and explain the point that unethical conduct is, through the action of many mechanisms, self-defeating or even self-destructive over the long run. It sounds old fashioned to say it, but only the soil of ethical goodness can nurture the human qualities necessary for people to work together well over the long haul.

The Basic Virtues

What are the basic virtues that allow people to work together well? Recall that we are thinking of the virtues as moral strengths, strengths of character that aid us in healthy, appropriate self-development and harmonious relationships with the people around us. Aristotle's list of virtues contains some items not usually thought of in connection with ethics at all. But it's important to see that there is no isolated domain of the ethical out of touch with other aspects of our lives.

The virtues are always understood in connection with some conception of the good life, some ideal of proper human success and flourishing. In the ancient Homeric past of Greece, the dominant ideal tended to be that of the hero facing a contest or battle, or the warrior-king triumphant over adversity. Many of the characteristics associated with that ideal would then be qualities that we still count as virtues, such as bravery, honor, and fidelity. In battle, strength was had by those who were brave, those who could trust their comrades, and those who would stay the course.

By Aristotle's time, the ideal of human living had come to be associated with the more stable social and political structures of at least quasi-democratic governance known as the polis, or city-state, of which Athens was a model. The ideal human being was the good free citizen of the polis, and the virtues were identified as those qualities facilitating harmonious and productive citizenship in such a context.

The Virtues According to Aristotle	
Courage	Good Temper
Temperance	Friendliness
Liberality	Truthfulness
Magnificence	Wittiness
Pride	Justice

I know that, confronted with this particular list, you're bound to be asking yourself, "Am I magnificent enough?" In my own life, I admit that this one could always use a little work.

For Aristotle, the quality called magnificence comes into play with the ability to do things on a grand scale when called for, something like the aesthetic and moral capacity to do things right when a dramatic gesture or bold enterprise is needed. Aristotle saw this virtue as one that would contribute to the overall good health and general welfare of the best social project of human living. Remember that for the ancient Greeks of prior centuries, as well as for Aristotle, the virtues were thought of as those qualities generally preparing a person for the fullest, most perfect participation in the ideal of the good life, and most conducive to the sort of success embodied in that ideal.

> *If a superior man abandons virtue, how can he fulfill the require-ments of that name?* —CONFUCIUS

Aristotle's list of the virtues thus was drawn up with the requirements of superior democratic citizenship and maximal human flourishing in mind. In any democracy, as in any organization making the most of its members' talents, participants must have the courage to speak their minds and follow their consciences. Thus, for Aristotle, as for his predecessors, courage is identified as a virtue. Friendliness oils the gears of social interaction, as does the attribute of wittiness, a quality we might not think of nowadays in connection with morality at all, but clearly one conducive to enjoying and benefiting from the company of others while engaged in any challenging enterprise. The moderation of speech and action known as temperance allows people to live more harmoniously together. And, likewise, all the other virtues identified by Aristotle would contribute to the sort of joint enterprise that Athenian democracy aspired to be.

A more modern list of human virtues might also contain, in no particular order, many or all of the following terms:

kindness	decency
honesty	modesty
loyalty	humility
sincerity	openness
reliability	cheerfulness
trustworthiness	amiability
benevolence	tolerance
thoughtfulness	reasonableness
sensitivity	tactfulness
helpfulness	gracefulness
cooperativeness	liveliness
civility	magnanimity
empathy	persistence
prudence	resourcefulness
boldness	coolheadedness
warmth	hospitality
politeness	creativity
hopefulness	faithfulness
altruism	love
harmony	balance
consistency	commitment
integrity	dignity
enthusiasm	humor
insightfulness	perspicacity
steadfastness	resiliency
thrift	self-discipline

You may think of other virtues not listed here. A human being is a multifaceted creature with many possible virtues, or character strengths, personal properties that promote spiritual health and social harmony, qualities that fit us for sustainable success and happiness together. The point is not so much to come up with an exhaustive inventory of the virtues as it is to understand the root nature of all these qualities. They are all meant to be characteristics that aid us in living well together, in making a positive difference in this life, and in becoming the best people that we can be. They are all attitudes, habits, or dispositions of character conducive to living a meaningful life in the best and deepest of ways. They are to be thought of as either causal contributors to, or else constituents of, genuine human happiness. They are part of a good life. And they are foundations of good business.

The Nature of Wisdom and Virtue

So we have virtue in general and we have the particular virtues. But we don't have both wisdom in general and the particular wisdoms. There are intellectual virtues. Some of them are listed. And they are habits of mind conducive to wisdom, often produced by wisdom, but also in turn productive of it. We do talk of bits of wisdom, pieces of wisdom, or even glimmers of wisdom. These are individual insights, and their inventory by enumeration is every bit as impossible as a complete listing of all the truths there are, and maybe even more so, since there are perhaps insights, illuminations, or deliverences of wisdom that can never fully be put into words. Some perhaps cannot even be named by words. But they can guide us instinctively, intuitively, and accurately.

Have you ever thought about the fact that the great philosopher Socrates had a student named Plato, and that Plato had a student named Aristotle? Is it just an amazing coincidence that sometimes great teachers have great students who themselves turn into great teachers, and so on? A British scientist, physician, and philosopher, Michael Polanyi, thinks it's no coincidence at all. He has suggested that this pattern can be found in many domains of human activity. Given the right context of intimate and sustained association, greatness gives rise to greatness.

> *A single conversation across the table with a wise man is better than ten years' mere study of books.* —HENRY WADSWORTH LONGFELLOW

The old master-apprentice model of education captured a powerful truth. You have a much better chance of becoming great if you hang around with great people. Polanyi cites the Nobel Prize winners in science whose students went on to win Nobels themselves. He insists that it's not just politics. Since the published results of the work of these great scientists are available for other researchers all around the world to read, why is it that something special is picked up by the students who actually worked and talked with the master all day in the lab? Polanyi suggests that we convey to those around us insights, knowledge, and wisdom that can never fully be put into words. He calls this "personal knowledge" or "tacit knowledge." This kind of wisdom can't always be captured in a catchy aphorism, an epigrammatic witticism, a slogan for living, or a five-second sound bite, but it is nonetheless real and powerful.

Just as wisdom can't always be captured in words, neither can virtue always be laid out in rules. Principles may guide us in the right direction, but when crunch time comes, morality is not a matter of just automatically applying the right rules or principles.

We all sometimes wish that there could be something like a moral pocket calculator. You'd punch in a problem, and enter a system of ethics—"Let's see, enter Problem: I've-received-this-nice-gift-from-a-potential-supplier-and-if-I-accept-it,-I-may-compromise-the-appearance-or-even-the-reality-of-my-decision-making-process,-but-if-I-refuse-it,-I-may-insult-a-possible-business-partner. OK, enter ethical system: Judeo-Christian ethics . . . no, I feel like a little something Chinese today . . . how about Confucian ethics?"—and out pops a solution. Of course, it can never be that simple. Ethics is not algorithmic; it's never just a matter of calculating from rules. It's more like a skill or even an art.

> *Wisdom and virtue are like the two wheels of a cart.*
> —JAPANESE PROVERB

Wisdom and virtue together compose the fertile soil within which moral character, ethical culture, and a positive corporate spirit can grow. If we want to cultivate the moral dimension in our organizations, as well as in our relationships and in our own lives, we need to respect and nurture both wisdom and virtue at each of those levels. But a question can arise here. If wisdom can sometimes be so elusive, then how can it be purposively cultivated in our lives and in our organizations? For that matter, if virtue is so manifold and like a skill, or an art, how can it be captured and conveyed and encouraged? In other words, appreciating the crucial role of wisdom and virtue, how can we create a more ethical climate for our lives and for all our joint endeavors?

The answers to these questions, fortunately, are much simpler than you might think.

Three Keys to Character and Culture

I believe there are three basic ways of cultivating wisdom and virtue in our lives, and by consequence in our organizations. When we understand and act on these three simple strategies, we position ourselves and those around us to make the best, most ethical decisions and to experience fulfillment and happiness in our work.

Moral Mentors

Key Number One: Network with Sages

Hang around with wise people. Associate as much as you can with people of admirable character and proven sagacity. We become like the people we're around. I've heard it said that if you're married to a person long enough, you begin to look like your spouse. I find this view fascinating, but for some reason my wife is horrified by the prospect. Of course, I'm only joking, but the point here is very serious.

> *Every man becomes, to a certain degree, what the people he generally converses with are.*
>
> —PHILIP DORMER STANHOPE, EARL OF CHESTERFIELD

The apparent malleability of the human personality is truly extraordinary. As we can pick up greatness from associating with masters, so also we can weaken and degrade our sensibilities by a contrary form of congress.

This is why the great thinkers have always encouraged us to avoid bad company. Bad company corrupts. And absolute scoundrels corrupt absolutely.

> *Avarice will stick to you as long as you keep company with a mean and avaricious man. Conceit will stick to you as long as you associate with an arrogant man. You'll never get rid of cruelty while you share lodgings with a torturer. You will inflame your lusts if you fraternize with adulterers. If you wish to be rid of your vices you must steer well clear of examples set by the vicious.* —SENECA

In many organizations, there is a lot of talk about "mentoring," but this is usually understood in a fairly narrow, political and technical way. A younger associate is encouraged to pick up hints, tips, and techniques for getting things done from a more experienced colleague. Mentoring is viewed as expediting institutional enculturation and raising the neophyte's learning curve. It's not often enough understood as a way of conveying wisdom throughout an organization. It's not enough to take a new employee and show him the ropes. He may just go and hang himself. Mentoring should be viewed as a way of cultivating good decision makers. It should be put firmly into the service of goodness in the business. People need good training. But more importantly, we need good people.

If you are in an executive position, then make sure you hire good people and do whatever you can to apprentice them to wiser people, because by association with sages they will catch the spirit of those values that alone can move an organization further along the road of enduring excellence. Good people make for good organizations. And good organizations provide the right conditions for good decision making.

The Importance of Small Details

Key Number Two: Take Care in Little Things

The poet Samuel Taylor Coleridge wrote, "There is nothing insignificant." We should all make this a motto hung over our desks. The moral dimension begins in little things. The ethics of decision making turns on little things. Everything we do matters. And it all adds up.

> *He who would do good to another must do it in Minute Particulars.*
> *General Good is the plea of the scoundrel, hypocrite, and flatterer.*
> —WILLIAM BLAKE

Too many people in high places talk big about ethics, and morality, and virtue, and goodness, but do not practice these qualities when they interact day-to-day with the people who work for them. There are far too many people who want to increase the general weal of the world without doing the unglamorous and sometimes inconvenient work of, for example, responding in kindness to a coworker during a time of stress. The little kindnesses, the small decencies, form the foundation for truly magnificent things. Without them, nothing of lasting value among human beings can be created.

> *Sometimes when I consider what tremendous consequences come from little things—a chance word, a tap on the shoulder, or a penny dropped on a newsstand—I am tempted to think . . . there are no little things.*
> —RALPH WALDO EMERSON

If you asked me what the single most important thing is that I've ever learned in years of studying ethics, I would not hesitate in responding. If I could pass on only one thing I've discovered in the realm of wisdom and virtue, this would be it. It's an insight that goes back at least as far as the ancient Greek philosophers. It is almost a theme song for Aristotelianism, and all the subsequent dynamic philosophies. It is simple, and it is profound. It can be put in a single sentence, and should be written on our hearts as well as on our minds. It is this:

> Whenever you make a decision, whenever you act,
> you are never just doing, you are always becoming.

Every decision, and every action, has implications not only out there in the world but in our innermost beings. It's like throwing a stone into a pond. It never just sinks, but creates ripples. In the same way, anything you do, however small, creates ripples in your character. It makes it a little more likely that you'll act in the same way again. Patterns are formed, however subtly. Habits of mind and of conduct begin to take root. And you change, however slightly, from what you previously were.

In everything we do, however large or small, we should always be asking ourselves: "In doing this, am I becoming the kind of person I want to be?" One of the greatest dangers in life is the ever-present threat of self-deception. We often believe we can do something, "just this one time," without its having any implications for who we are. But there are no exceptions to this process. We can never take a holiday away from moral significance. Everything we do forms us, molds us, shapes us into the people we are becoming.

> So build we up the being that we are. —WILLIAM WORDSWORTH

In his insightful little book, *Leadership Is an Art*, Max De Pree makes the important point that, like the people who make up an organization, every organization itself is constantly in a state of becoming. What a company, or department, or office, or association, or family becomes is a direct result of what the people in that structure are becoming. Our actions on even the smallest scale thus affect not only our own trajectories through the world but the characters of our organizations. We owe it to others as well as to ourselves always to take care in little things so that the process of becoming that we are engaged in will have positive results of personal and organizational strength.

Corporate spirit is a dynamic thing, and is created day to day by the actions of everyone in the organization, from the front lines to the executive suites. Nothing is irrelevant. Everything matters. It's crucially important to display as well as to preach consistency in ethical conduct everywhere in the company. The stories we tell to co-workers, the things we praise, the actions we reward, all contribute toward establishing the right or the wrong kind of corporate spirit. Little things make all the difference. And this is the basis for the second key to character and culture, which is a key to wisdom and virtue.

Moral Imagination

Key Number Three: Cultivate a Perceptive Imagination

It's amazing to me how little is typically said about the imagination when ethics is being discussed. I've come to believe that within the moral dimension of human experience, nothing is more important than developing a lively, vivid, and perceptive imagination.

Have you even done a moral audit of your life? I did exactly this for the first time a few years ago, and I was surprised by the results. I made a list of everything I could remember that I had ever done during my late teen and adult years that I had later come to regret as ethically wrong. It was not too long a list, but it did have enough entries to give me pause. I then asked myself whether there was anything that all, or most, of those situations had in common, and the answer I arrived at was that in every case I had failed to imagine vividly and perceptively the full consequences of my actions for other people as well as for myself. I had put blinders on my moral imagination and had seen in advance only those consequences that I wanted to see. I had proved myself a master of self-deception and rationalization.

> *The easiest thing of all is to deceive one's self; for what a man wishes, he generally believes to be true.* —DEMOSTHENES

But when I thought about this, I came to realize that most human beings are masters of self-deception. We have an uncanny knack for selective attention and narrowly self-centered focus. Whenever you face a difficult decision and see yourself inclined toward the path of your own immediate self-interest, you should always beware of the possibility of self-deception and rationalization. I wish we all had built in warning buzzers and lights that would flash whenever a situation arose that set us up for self-deceived thinking and selective attention. Sadly, we don't. But we do have something else that can work just as well if we develop it properly: the power of imagination.

> *The great instrument of moral good is the imagination.* —PERCY BYSSHE SHELLEY

One of the most powerful aids for wisdom and virtue is a properly developed moral imagination, an enhanced capacity for envisioning how our decisions and actions impinge on other people as well as our own process of personal becoming, in morally appropriate and inappropriate ways. The role of great literature, art, theater, and film in moral development has always been to feed and spark our imaginative abilities to perceive the ethical implications of whatever we contemplate doing. Any society in which the moral imagination is not fed is a society in trouble.

We need to help the people around us to cultivate a vivid vision for the virtues of our organizations and the moral power of doing things right. How do our decisions affect customers and suppliers? It's hard for us to imagine this well if we don't really know the customers and the vendors we work with. And we can't know them if we hardly ever see them. This is one reason why it's so important to give people a chance to get off campus, out of their offices, and out of the building, to visit the people they serve.

Whenever manufacturing or design people actually make site visits and see firsthand how customers are using their products, they develop a new insightful imaginative feel for the needs of the customer, and sometimes the plight of the customer. They come face to face with what works well and what doesn't work as it should. They hear from other real people what they like and don't like about the product, what they need and what they'd really like to have if it were just possible. When the end user becomes a face and a voice, a genuine, three-dimensional human being, it is much more difficult to ignore his or her interests and needs. This is a natural impetus for good decision making, with the customer's interests at heart.

> It is by imagination that we cross over the differences between ourselves and other beings and thus learn compassion, forbearance, mercy, forgiveness, sympathy, and love—the virtues without which neither we nor the world can survive.　　　—WENDELL BERRY

To develop wisdom and virtue, we need to cultivate a perceptive imagination on two different levels. First, we need imagination on a small scale. We need empathy. You can't know how you would want to be treated if you were in another person's shoes unless you can imagine what it would be like to be in his shoes. It is hard to develop empathy in a robust form without getting to know in concrete and detailed ways the people with whom we need to empathize. One of the most important business commandments then should be: Know thy customer. And its equal should be: Know thy associate. Empathy is a virtue, a habit or disposition of imaginative identification that must be applied consistently in your life to be well developed. It is just as important to be empathetic to people within your organization as it is to be imaginatively attuned to those on the outside whom you serve. Service and empathy must flow through an organization first if they are to flow out unimpeded to those with whom the organization does business. What happens in the inner circle flows on to those outside.

> *A fellow feeling makes one wondrous kind.* —DAVID GARRICK

We also need to cultivate imagination on a large scale, a vivid vision for our lives and our businesses. We need an imaginative conception of what we are doing, a big picture for the contribution we are making to the world. We need a map with coordinates to guide us in our concrete day-to-day decisions. If we don't know who we are or where we're going, how can we possibly know exactly what we should do today, and tomorrow? Vision is fundamental for ethical success in the world.

The overall imaginative vision that we have for the work we are doing serves as something like a basic template for all our other work-related thinking. Blaise Pascal pointed out in the middle of the seventeenth century, "Our whole duty is to think as we ought." From our most fundamental forms of thinking flow our attitudes, our emotions, our decisions, and our actions. With a powerful ethical vision directing all our other thoughts, we don't need long lists of rules to guide us. We are both informed and inspired to do what is right.

Seeing the Big Picture

How do we cultivate a big picture vision for our work? By looking at what we do in the noblest possible light. By attending to what we create, what products, services, structures, and overall goods we provide for others, as well as for ourselves. We need to think through on a global scale how the small things we do day to day may ripple out into the world and accomplish great good in the lives of others, in both direct and indirect ways.

> *Thought constitutes man's greatness.* —PASCAL

We need to practice focusing our thoughts on the dignity of what we do when we are at our best, and we need to help those who work with us to do the same thing. I was visiting a business not too long ago that used a simple vision-building technique to great effect. Every employee entered the building through the same set of doors and passed down a hallway decorated with photographs of great moments in the company's history over a span of a hundred years. That small entrance gallery gave everyone the feeling of being a part of something big, something that mattered in the community, something they could be proud of and inspired by as they confronted the difficulties and opportunities of the day.

Pep talks inspire only if they ennoble. Motivational messages never have long-term impact unless they engage the moral imagination and spur it on to good work. The imagination is the deepest fount of motivation in human nature. When it is formed by a moral vision, it goads and guides us to good effect.

Whenever something goes wrong, debrief the people involved. Get their imaginations in gear, and help them to appreciate the magnitude of the problem. Likewise, when something goes very right, tell the story around the organization. Get people's imaginations going in a positive way. A perceptive imagination is the most powerful source and support we have for the encouragement and cultivation of both wisdom and virtue. It will help keep us on the straight ethical path to long-term excellence.

> *Even if I should not follow the straight road because of its straightness, I would follow it because I have found by experience that when all is said and done it is generally the happiest and the most useful.*
> —MICHEL EYQUEM DE MONTAIGNE

Network with sages. Take care in little things. Cultivate a perceptive imagination. It's not rocket science, but that's just fine; we're not rockets. These are the simple keys to the fundamental realities of human nature that lie beneath all the apparent complexities of life, and all the twists and turns of the moral dimension. With their assistance we can cultivate genuine goodness in our lives and our organizations and in this way build the sort of positive corporate spirit necessary for long-term business excellence and human happiness at work.

IV
UNITY

10

The Spiritual Dimension at Work

The fourth universal dimension of human experience is the spiritual dimension, that aspect of our nature which strives for unity or ultimate connectedness. Spiritual unity is then the fourth foundation for sustainable excellence in all human organizations and enterprises. We'll see that this final dimension is the proper culmination of the other three, both undergirding and overarching them.

Spiritual unity may be the last thing that comes to mind when most businesspeople think and talk about strengthening their companies. As Socrates said, it seems that the least important things we think and talk about the most, and the most important, we think about and talk about the least. It's essential to think and talk about the spiritual dimension of work.

Every human being has four spiritual needs that must be respected and nurtured every day. It's not enough for us to take care of those needs just at home, at church or synagogue, or in private meditation or personal prayer. The deep needs of the human spirit go far beyond these limited contexts.

Our spiritual needs must be met in the work we do, or that work will be like a trek through the desert, exhausting rather than fulfilling, part of our plight rather than part of our purpose. Work can be satisfying and meaningful only if it contributes to meeting our most basic spiritual needs.

> *Greatness is a spiritual condition.* —MATTHEW ARNOLD

The Depth of the Spirit

When I talk about the spiritual, the spirit, or spirituality, I am not necessarily talking about anything distinctly religious at all. We all have a spiritual dimension to our lives, regardless of what our religious orientation is, and even regardless of whether we think of ourselves as religious beings at all. Southern Baptists, Presbyterians, Catholics, Jews, Hindus, and Muslims, as well as agnostics and atheists, all share a spiritual dimension to their experience, whether they recognize it as such or not.

Spirituality is fundamentally about two things: depth and connectedness. The more spiritually developed a person is, the more that individual will see a depth of meaning and significance under the surface appearances of things in our world. The less spiritually attuned a person is, the more likely that man or woman is to mistake illusory appearances for realities.

Plato had a great metaphor for this. Imagine a number of human beings living their lives in a huge cave, chained down and facing a wall. Behind them there is a fire, and between that fire and their backs, various objects move by, their shadows being cast on the wall. Those imprisoned in the cave and looking at the wall mistake these shadows for realities. And so they pass their lives.

What would happen, though, Plato asks us, if one of the prisoners broke free of those chains, turned around, and made his way out of the cave into the great light of the world beyond? He might at first be blinded by the light but would eventually be able to see realities previously unavailable to view. Now imagine this escapee returning to the cave to tell his fellows what he has seen and try to convince them to break away themselves. What would their reaction be? Would he be believed? Would he even be understood?

Plato was convinced that most human beings in our world live their lives like those cave dwellers, imprisoned in a realm of deceptive illusions and shadows of reality. The philosopher, Plato suggested, is an individual who breaks his chains and ventures out into the world of real truth. When he brings his news from the realm of genuine illumination back into the cave, he is not always understood or believed. And that should be no surprise.

Freeing ourselves of illusions is always a difficult task. But it is the one true path to meaning and fulfillment.

One of the greatest challenges of our times is that too many of our business and political leaders are trapped in the cave. Busy mistaking shadows for realities, they fail to make connections crucial for finding their way out. Plato believed that this will continue until our leaders become philosophers, discover what we really need, and bring those deeper insights into our organizational lives with both courage and persistence.

> *Cities will have no respite from evil, my dear Glaucon, nor will the human race, I think, unless philosophers rule as kings in the cities, or those whom we now call kings and rulers genuinely and adequately study philosophy, until, that is, political power and philosophy coalesce, and the various natures of those who now pursue one to the exclusion of the other are forcibly debarred from doing so.*
>
> —SOCRATES, ACCORDING TO PLATO

Think about how amazingly modern Plato's ideas are. How many people mistakenly worship and pursue celebrity or wealth, thinking that these things alone will make them happy? How many people fear what will never actually happen, or what, even if it did come about, could never really hurt them? In times of great corporate or social change, the shadows that pass over us tend to freeze many people in fear of their futures. Plato would want us to free ourselves of these illusions and see more deeply the realities in life.

The Example of Brother Jeff

Too many people mistake the surface appearances of their jobs for the real thing. But the spiritual depth latent in any job that is productive of any sort of good is almost incalculable. Let me give you a particularly striking example of this. One of the most spiritually attuned people I have ever met is the custodian of Decio Faculty Hall at the University of Notre Dame. His name is Weldon Jeffries, or "Brother Jeff" to his friends, which includes nearly everyone he's ever met. What is a janitor's job? He sweeps up, vacuums floors, empties trash cans, cleans bathrooms, washes windows, and occasionally fixes something that's broken. At least that's the surface. But it's only the surface. The depth is different. At least it is the way Brother Jeff does it. He creates, cares for, and maintains an environment in which people can do good work. He enhances people's working lives, day-to-day. He loves and nurtures human beings. He is a custodian of souls.

Does this sound a little extreme? It's completely true. In an office building full of hundreds of Ph.D.s, whenever anyone faces a personal challenge, has trouble at home, is bothered by any sort of worry or fear, or just needs a spark of renewed energy, they easily discover that the wisest course of action is to seek out the one man in the building who didn't graduate from high school, Brother Jeff. He whistles while he works, he sings, he greets everyone with a big smile and a kind word: "How are you today, my friend?" An otherwise dour face may brighten and respond, "Fine, Jeff, and how are you?" The inevitable answer? "Everything's pretty!" A conversation then may or may not ensue, on almost any topic imaginable. But if it does, it always ends with a hearty send-off: "You have yourself a great day, my friend!"

Brother Jeff especially likes to greet faculty members he knows well with half a biblical verse, hoping for the remainder in response. I recall with great pleasure the first cold grim morning he turned to me in the hallway, as I had just entered the building, with the words, "Brother Morris, this is the day the Lord hath made . . ." and I was able to respond immediately, "Let us rejoice and be glad in it!" to which he boomed an enthusiastic "Amen!" I remember smiling big, shaking my head in amazement, and having a much better morning than I otherwise would have experienced.

Weldon Jeffries seems to understand the real importance of what he does. Nobody would ever even dream of ranking Jeff as among the least important people in the building. To anyone with any discernment whatsoever, he very well may be one of the most important individuals in that building. In my many years of working within the sphere of his influence, I gradually came to realize that he may in fact be one of the very most important people on the whole campus of the University of Notre Dame.

> No race can prosper till it learns that there is as much dignity in tilling a field as in writing a poem.　　　　—BOOKER T. WASHINGTON

Brother Jeff is happy in his work not because he's unaware of the problems of the world, or without problems of his own. He's a thinker, as ready with a disquisition on politics and current events as he is quick with a smile and a good word for anyone who's down. And he's not unacquainted with troubles. I have seen him serve his fellow man and woman as his own beloved brother lay dying. And two weeks before the writing of these words, his twenty-six-year-old son was gunned down in South Bend, the innocent victim of a drive-by shooting. But Jeff brings a spiritual depth to life that gives him a powerful perspective on death. The words of forgiveness and love that he spoke at his son's funeral were not only illuminating but even life-changing for many who attended. In the midst of his own most challenging moments, he reaches out and makes a difference for good in the lives of those around him.

Spirituality is all about depth, the depth beneath the surface, the meaning and significance that don't always meet the eye. It's about plugging into a source of personal energy and positive hope only to be found outside the cave. At work, it's the ability to see and do the real job at hand in a way that doesn't usually show up in the official job description. And it's the capacity to show others this extra depth that they might otherwise miss.

The surface realities of our jobs are a little like the foam on a glass of beer. It's an unsatisfied person who just sucks off the foam and never drinks deeply of the beer itself. If we could all enjoy a deeper view of what life is all about and, connected to that, a deeper view of the work we do; if we could free ourselves of those illusions that dance across the surface of our daily endeavors; and if, as a consequence, we could experience the positive energy that comes from living a robustly spiritual approach to life day to day, we would find a much greater sense of satisfaction and fulfillment in our work. And, connected with that, I am convinced that as a result we would do better work, in the small and sometimes deceptively unexciting details, as well as in the larger challenges we face.

> *No task, rightly done, is truly private. It is part of the world's work.*
>
> —WOODROW WILSON

One of the things executives, managers, or supervisors should always have in mind is the ongoing need to help the people around them to have this deeper view of their jobs individually as well as of what the organization as a whole is doing in the world. And, of course, managers and executives won't be able to impart this unless they themselves feel it first. But this is exactly the problem in many companies.

The higher in an organization a person is, the more temptations there are to lose track of the spiritual significance of what is going on in favor of the numbers-and-prestige game we are all taught to play. But money, rank, and external accomplishment are not enough to satisfy. It is the internal orientation of the heart that makes all the difference in the world. What are we doing? And how do we do it?

Weldon Jeffries does not just augment his job as custodian with extra duties as a caretaker of souls. He does every aspect of his job with soul. He pours himself into every task, however small, with an extraordinary spirit. And he reaps what he sows. He gets out of each task a return of joy proportionate to the exuberance, care, and loving attentiveness he puts into it. He's no actor dramatizing the ordinary. He is a fully spiritual person who is able to see and act on the truly extraordinary potential and significance buried deep within the most mundane things lying all around. He not only sees the depths, he lives the depths. And there is no job productive of good that lacks those depths.

It's said that life is either a daring adventure, or nothing. It's up to each of us to decide if we're satisfied with being chained in the cave, staring at shadows on the wall, or whether we'll insist on seeing and living fully as we go about our daily work. The spirit with which we approach our work will determine in large part what that work really is.

> *It is the spiritual always that determines the material.*
> —THOMAS CARLYLE

In the seventeenth century, the great mathematician and scientist Blaise Pascal suggested that there are three orders of reality: the physical realm, or the order of the body; the intellectual realm, or the order of the mind; and the spiritual realm, or the order of the heart. Too often we live in just one or two of these realms and neglect many things that are very important for a full life. We live and think physically. What matters is matter, and all the quantifications of matter—the buildings, the cars, the houses, the jets, and all the numbers: the orders, market share, margins, profits, and ratios we read like tea leaves to keep score and learn of the future. Or we live and think intellectually, as if concepts and ideas are everything. We reason, we argue, we plan, scheme, and persuade. We think our way through the day. The realm or order we are most likely to neglect, says Pascal, is fundamentally the most important for everything that we do: the realm of the spiritual, the order of the heart. It is ultimately the source of sustainable excellence and enduring joy. But we often crowd it out because of busyness or stress in the physical realm or in the intellectual domain. And we thus rob ourselves of what we most deeply need.

We don't typically sink our intellectual and emotional roots deep enough into reality. So in times of surface drought we have no source of nurture, strength, and refreshment. The most spiritually developed people who have ever lived have had great advice for all of us. Put your roots down deep. Anchor yourself way down at the ultimate foundations. Make contact with the Ground of all Being. Draw from the deep springs. This is the only source of abiding balance and harmony, motivation and hope, or fulfillment and satisfaction. This is the source of the peace and equanimity the ancient Stoics sought as the direct result of an act of will. But as the most spiritual thinkers have discovered, it rather is a matter of the heart. It comes from depth.

Connectedness and the Spirit

The heart of spirituality is connectedness. The ultimate target of the spiritual dimension is unity: connectedness, or intimate integration, between our thoughts and our actions, between our beliefs and emotions, between ourselves and others, between human beings and the rest of nature, between all of nature and nature's source. Unlimited connectedness. Ultimate unity.

Unfortunately, we live in a time of great disunity and disconnectedness between people and their communities, among races, within families, between ordinary citizens and their political processes and representatives, between people in governmenal roles, between departments in the same company, between teachers and principals, doctors and nurses, practitioners and insurers, management and labor. Alienation and the adversarial mindset are everywhere. This is not a spiritual state of being. It is, rather, the antithesis of what spirituality aspires to realize.

Indian philosophy and Hindu thought stress the deep oneness of all things. Judaism proclaims the importance of brotherly unity. The New Testament says of Jesus the Christ, "In him, all things hold together." Even developments in modern physics return over and over to the theme of the fundamental constitutive unity of all things in this world. But if we don't experience such unity in our offices, or in our families, or even in our own personal consciousness on a pragmatic, everyday level, then what's gone wrong? And what can we do about it?

To see the connectedness that does exist all around us, beneath surface appearances, we need to free ourselves of the illusion of utter individual autonomy. The modern world encourages us to seek our own fortune, discover our own talents, and make for ourselves a future. The bookstores of America are full of self-help books and psychological manuals for self-healing and self-mastery. We've been encouraged to think predominantly, if not exclusively, about our individual needs and wants. At best, we think of our most immediate families as a unit whose welfare is, at least in principle, relatively independent of the fortunes and futures of all the rest of the people around us.

It's always easy in life to focus on the more immediate parts of an over-arching process, or encompassing entity, and neglect the whole. We focus on our careers and don't sufficiently consider them in the context of the whole that is our life, or we cultivate a relationship without considering the impact it may have on the entirety of what we value and love. We confront a decision and focus on the problem at hand without thinking through the connections that hold between a specific situation and the overall set of relationships that holds it in place.

Fragmentation, compartmentalization, and a false sense of autonomy are modern diseases of thought and feeling. We too easily overlook the insight of the old African proverb reminding us that it never rains on just one house. What affects one of us affects many of us. We are all interconnected in our past, in our present, and in our future. We are essentially social beings who depend on community even when we neglect to recognize this fundamental rootedness.

> *Your own safety is at stake when your neighbor's wall is ablaze.*
> —HORACE

To fail to see the ultimate interconnectedness of our prospects is both extremely dangerous and all too common.

In everything we do, considerations of context and connection should guide us. The architect Eliel Saarinen offered an insightful piece of advice that far transcends the scope of its originally intended application: "Always design a thing by considering it in its next larger context—a chair in a room, a room in a house, a house in an environment, an environment in a city plan." This should be a blueprint we use everywhere in our lives. Everything we do should be thought through in the context of its next larger environment, and that in its next larger environment, and so on. With this in mind, we may sometimes find it easier to compromise our own personal preferences on one issue for the sake of a larger, ongoing relationship. We may be able to give up a point or a measure of profit on one occasion for the sake of the bigger picture. We might be more understanding toward a coworker if we take context into consideration. And we may be more sensitive about breaking a connection when we understand the overall importance of connectedness to what we are able to accomplish.

Matters of the spirit are, and should always be, connected with concerns of truth, beauty, and goodness. Truth is the most resilient and lasting tie for connecting people and organizations, if the truth is always spoken in love. Alliances built on falsehood can never last. But for the truth to have its most powerful impact in a positive direction, it should always be embraced and used within the overall governing context of a concern for ultimate unity. Hard truths can and should sometimes be spoken, but never just to destroy, always also to build. Likewise, beauty is an element of spiritual connectedness. When we connect our work with meanings and purposes attached to our deepest aspirations, we find the result to be beautiful in one of the deepest possible senses. Additionally, environments of beauty for life and work make it more likely that activities within those environments will inspire and bear fruit on a spiritual level.

Finally, goodness is conducive to the needs of the spirit, as we shall see in the following chapter. The spiritual perspective, likewise, most reliably tends to the creation of goodness. And much more along these lines could be said. The greatest beauty in human relations comes about through the proper integration of truth and goodness in unity. So there are deep and multiply intertwined connections between and among the respective targets of all the four basic dimensions of human experience. But the greatest of these is the spiritual, itself the dimension of depth and connection.

We should always be thinking of connections in our business dealings and decision making—connecting our talents and experiences with things we can do for the business; connecting our efforts with those of other people, associates we normally work around, and people in other departments with whom we might creatively interact; and finally, building positive connections with suppliers, vendors, and clients, connections that will take us into the future with the sort of collaborative effort that our world economy now makes necessary.

> *Mankind has become so much one family that we cannot insure our own prosperity except by insuring that of everyone else. If you wish to be happy yourself, you must resign yourself to seeing others also happy.* —BERTRAND RUSSELL

11

Uniqueness and Union

The four universal spiritual needs felt by human beings are both simple and powerful. We all have a deep need for a sense of:

1. *Uniqueness* as individuals;

2. *Union* with something greater than the self;

3. *Usefulness* to others; and

4. *Understanding* about our lives and work.

When these needs are respected and met, we're capable of experiencing deep fulfillment and personal satisfaction in our lives and in our work. When they're not being met, our activities drain us of our vital forces and eventually alienate us deeply.

The Need for Uniqueness

We all need to feel unique, special, different in a positive way, set apart and distinctive as the individuals that we are. We're not exactly like anyone else, and we all need to feel that this is recognized and affirmed. This is the first of our four basic spiritual needs.

> *Anybody who is any good is different from anybody else.*
>
> —FELIX FRANKFURTER

This morning I went to school with my children; it was Orientation Day for new students and parents, as well as for all seventh and ninth graders. As I watched the middle schoolers and beginning high schoolers enter the gymnasium where we were all congregating, I was vividly reminded of my own student days, and of the new-school jitters. Some of the first-time students walked in very slowly and hesitantly, looking a little lost and worried. Others, obviously veteran ninth graders, swaggered in with attitude, and, occasionally, an entourage. Small groups gathered outside. The alternative-rock-crowd poets on one side, the preppies down the sidewalk. Friends found friends and stuck together as if their lives depended on it. No one wanted to be alone or to feel alone. From what I could see, every young student on that campus needed to be recognized and accepted as a unique person. The great fear, almost palpable around that building on this first morning of the new school year, was whether that would happen this year, in this place, and with these people.

On the surface, teenagers can sometimes appear as if they all want to look alike, act alike, and actually be alike, down to the smallest details, at least within the confines of some group with whom they identify. But a more penetrating analysis sees something else. Each of us wants to be noticed and appreciated by others. If we don't think we're in a position to wow the world at large, we'll pick a group of people among whom we think we likely can find this acceptance and affirmation of our uniqueness. And then we'll become in many ways like the members of that group, adopting their dress, their mannerisms, and their language, hoping that this will gain us the level of acceptance that it usually takes for any other people to be in a position to get to know us in our real inner distinctiveness.

Unlike chameleons, we change colors not so that we won't be noticed but so that we'll be accepted enough by some group ultimately to be noticed, at least by its members. And if this is a group noticed and admired by others, their acceptance of us may gain us wider acceptance and perhaps even some of that wider admiration.

> *We must resemble each other a little in order to understand each other, but we must be a little different to love each other.*
>
> —PAUL GÉRALDY

The truth is that the dynamics of adolescence never leave us completely. And, of course, these qualities didn't just spring into operation when we turned twelve or thirteen. They were also, to different degrees, the dynamics of childhood. When my daughter, Sara, was eight years old, she used to come into the house on occasion and complain about the little girl across the street, "Daddy, Lindsay is copying off me! She does everything I do, and I can't get her to stop!"

I pointed out to Sara that Lindsay was just four and was trying to learn what it would be like to be eight. She wanted to be accepted by kids of an age that she would one day be. She was looking to Sara for acceptance and for affirmation. When at the Morris house, she was doing as the Morris kids did. And what Sara had failed to notice was that she, too, often copied the older middle school girls, who were themselves busy imitating the high schoolers, who were in turn emulating the college kids, who in various ways were copying those few adults they admired. In the animal kingdom, it's known as "imprinting." We subconsciously mimic those we're around. In human life, we do this not just to become like them but so that they will come to notice and like us for who we ourselves are.

Celebrating Each Person

Every member of our families, all our friends, and each person who works with us has this deep need to be noticed, recognized, and appreciated as special, as a unique individual. That's why so much of the business management literature has stressed in recent years the need to celebrate people's accomplishments on the job, in big and small ways. Let the people around you know that you appreciate them. Congratulate a colleague for a job well done. Compliment a coworker on a talent she distinctively has, for going beyond the call of duty, for creatively solving a problem, or even for just speaking out when something needed to be said. Younger associates benefit from the encouragement. Older colleagues appreciate the honor.

> *The desire for glory clings even to the best men longer than any other passion.*
> —CORNELIUS TACITUS

We all need this kind of positive notice. And we need to be given challenges at work that draw on our unique qualities and backgrounds. No two people have the same talents and the same experiences. We each have something different to offer, intellectually, physically, and creatively. An organization that doesn't recognize this and make use of it is missing a crucially important opportunity and squandering its most readily available resource.

> *The emerging economy is based on knowledge, imagination, curiosity, and talent. What if we could learn to tap the wonderful, rich differences among people? Wouldn't a corporation that could exploit the uniqueness of each of its 1,000 employees (or 10 or 10,000) be phenomenally powerful? Put negatively, isn't a corporation that doesn't figure out how to use the special curiosities of its people headed for trouble?* —TOM PETERS

A company president once told me that one day he realized that people in his offices really didn't know each other's unique backgrounds and experiences. They may have known each other's names, and an autobiographical detail here and there, but they really didn't know each other as people, and he suspected that this would inevitably inhibit the work they could do together. So he gathered everybody together for a Saturday in the park. They played games and had a picnic, but it all built up to a time of sitting around in a big circle. He passed out three-by-five cards and asked everyone present to write on their card one secret about themselves that they thought no one else at work knew but that they wouldn't mind other people knowing. Without signing their names, they all dropped the cards into a big box. Then they began to pull out cards, reading each secret out loud and trying to guess whose it was. The results were funny, informative, and sometimes astonishing. They all discovered buried talents in the group that they could draw upon in the future, talents they didn't know that these other people had.

If we don't know the uniqueness of the person next to us, we can't plug into that distinctiveness in any powerful and productive way. If we do get to know our associates better, we put ourselves into a position for appreciating who they are, how their perspectives and skills are different from ours, and then how we can most effectively collaborate in new and creative ways.

Distinctive Forms of Service

Be yourself if you would serve others. —HENRY VAN DYKE

It is only when we are in tune with our own individuality, comfortable with the best of our own uniqueness, that we are in a position best to serve others. The people around us don't need replicas of themselves, cooperative clones to echo their voices, however much this may sometimes seem to be exactly what they desire. We contribute best to any joint enterprise when we are unafraid of bringing our distinctive perspectives and talents to bear on that venture. Just as we should encourage others to bring forth their special gifts and knowledge, we ought ourselves to be always moving toward deeper and more comprehensive states of self-awareness, self-knowledge, and self-development, so that we can put ourselves in the best position for contributing what we alone might be able to bring to any project. Each of us has a history not quite like that of any other person. We've had special experiences, and we've built up distinctive sets of skills, skills of thought as well as of action. We can make the most of our daily opportunities only if we get to know well, and accustom ourselves to drawing upon, our own unique trajectories through life.

The history of every individual should be a Bible. —NOVALIS

Become a student of yourself as well as of other people. And be quick to affirm the positive differences that you find. That way, you put yourself into the best position to use your uniqueness in all your endeavors.

The Price of Ignoring Individuality

My wife has done a lot of volunteer work in public schools, taking the most unruly children out of their classrooms and giving them special attention. She has told me that respectful attention, love, caring, and positive reinforcement can make all the difference in the world in the behavior of an elementary-school-age child who had previously seemed incapable of learning and cooperating in the classroom. These children, who often receive no ongoing positive recognition of their uniqueness at home, come to demand some form of individual attention at school. If they can't get positive attention, they seem to feel that negative attention is better than no attention at all. So they disobey the teacher, steal other children's belongings, and start fights. And of course this pattern of need and behavior is not confined to elementary school, or to just the most troubled students.

At work our associates need to be noticed, acknowledged, recognized, and celebrated as the distinctive individuals they are. If we do not celebrate them in positive ways, they may be very tempted to celebrate themselves in negative ways, rewarding themselves with prizes that are not rightfully theirs for the taking. Unappreciated people feel little or no sense of loyalty or camaraderie toward those who are ignoring them, and very little responsibility. So office supplies disappear. Travel expenses aren't what they should be. Credit is not shared for a joint project. Corporate spirit plummets.

It doesn't take free trips to Disney World to turn this around. Small shows of appreciation, in word or deed, can make a huge difference, as my wife discovered in her work with troubled schoolchildren, and as many of us have seen in our business endeavors. People need love and appreciation. And anyone who feels that these have no place in business just doesn't really understand what business is ultimately about.

Of course, what applies within a business also holds just as strongly between businesses. Do you make your customers feel unique? How about suppliers? Every sales relationship, every consulting relationship, any business link whatsoever between individuals and between companies is a context for the cultivation of positive corporate spirit, in the original, broadest sense of the term. If that relationship is one in which the other person feels nurtured in his need for a sense of uniqueness, the relationship will be strengthened. Whenever we make the people around us feel special in positive ways, we ourselves benefit from the results. And this is not the fluff of psychobabble, it's the reality of human nature.

> *A people, it appears, may be progressive for a certain length of time, and then stop. When does it stop? When it ceases to possess individuality.*
>
> —JOHN STUART MILL

The philosopher John Stuart Mill perceived something very important. Not only do individual human beings need to have a sense of distinctiveness in themselves, groups of people working together in partnership for some form of good also need to carry in their minds and hearts a sense of distinctiveness as a group, a sense of a unique community. Members of a family need to feel good about themselves as a family. Citizens of a city, state, or nation need to feel positive about themselves as parties to a distinctive human enterprise. And employees of a company need an excitement or pride in what they distinctively do as a company. That's one reason why an advertisement, done right, is often almost as worthwhile for its effect on the people who work in the company as for its impact on customers and potential customers. It enhances a sense of company distinctiveness and importance. As long as we feel unique in what we do, we're in a position to be deeply motivated to grow and improve, to go beyond what is required, and to move forward to new levels of excellence.

The Need for Union

> No man is an island, entire of itself; every man is a piece of the continent.
> —JOHN DONNE

The second universal human spiritual need—our need to feel a sense of union with something greater than the self—may seem at first to pull in the opposite direction from our need to feel unique. We all need to feel that we belong. This is the power behind family life, as well as the lure of street gangs.

One former gang leader in California recently made an provocative statement. He said kids join gangs not primarily for the money derived from illegal activities; nor because they want access to readily available, illicit drugs; nor to get guns or be able to shoot people. Rather, it's because they have a deep need to feel as if they belong to something important, something bigger than the individual self. If this need were being met in other, more productive ways, perhaps gangs would not have such a pull in our inner cities.

Our need for a sense of union with something greater than the self is the power behind school spirit. As a professor at Notre Dame for fifteen years, I felt the nearly magical aura of the Notre Dame mystique, the sense of identity among all Fightin' Irish students, alumni, staff, and fans around the country. It's an unseen force that holds people together, and that charges the whole campus with a special energy. This is also the power behind patriotism, and one of the moving forces underlying the world's great religions. It can also be the foundation for powerful corporate spirit in any business context.

A director of human resources recently told me that he had gone through an unusual experience in trying to help his company, a very well known and highly respected computer manufacturer, articulate a statement of company-wide values. A small group was put in charge of coming up with a draft of the document, and to this end they began to meet once a week. On the first week they started to brainstorm about values that mattered to the way the company did business.

Somebody suggested individuality as an important value. It was written on the board, as everyone else nodded approval. Another associate suggested teamwork. Nods were seen all around as this too was written on the board. Other characteristics valued by the organization were named and duly noted, with apparently harmonious agreement all around the table. The process seemed much easier than anyone had expected. The blackboard was filled with terms for all sorts of values. And the group felt very good about their first day's work.

At the next meeting, something quite different happened. They began by reviewing the list of values they had compiled during that first session. The guy who had suggested teamwork the previous week raised a question about individuality. How could this really be a company value, he wondered, when too much encouragement of individualism can result in anarchy, with mavericks running all around doing what they want to do, regardless of what's generally judged to be good for the organization?

The person who had suggested individuality as a valued characteristic replied by impugning teamwork. He wondered how it could be a basic value of any business in need of creativity to encourage group-think, or the degree of conformity often tied up with "being a team player." The formerly harmonious group suddenly exploded into polarized disagreement. As objections and replies flew around the room, the human resources director came to realize that each side was actually misrepresenting, and even caricaturing, the other side's favored value concepts.

> *Plurality which is not reduced to unity is confusion; unity which does not depend on plurality is tyranny.* —BLAISE PASCAL

T. H. Huxley once stated that "If individuality has no play, society does not advance; if individuality breaks out of all bounds, society perishes." And what is true of a larger society is also true of the society that makes up your business, or your department. The individuality that any organization needs to value, nurture, and encourage is just that uniqueness we've been investigating. It's not the maverick mentality of total individual autonomy. That would indeed lead to the confusion of plurality Pascal warns against and the lawlessness Huxley sees as leading to any organization's demise. The proper form of individuality we need to value is rather that sense of self necessary for bringing creative contributions to all our partnerships and collaborations. We each have something to contribute to the greater enterprise, something that can't precisely be replicated by anyone else. If we don't encourage this sort of contributive individuality on the part of everyone around us, we lose the best use of the most important resources we have.

The teamwork that an organization should promote is not the herd mentality that leads people lemminglike in the wrong direction, stressing conformity and blind obedience to authoritarian orders. It is precisely the opposite, a state of mind and pattern of action in which individuals join their associates in doing things together that none of them could have accomplished alone. It is a mindset of personal responsibility to a group and enterprise, an individual initiative in the context of partnership, a sharing of values, vision, and resources, and an openness to and even eagerness for mutual correction, learning, and the reinforcement of support and encouragement. The best teams are groups of individual leaders bringing their talents, experiences, and energies together in creative ways in service to some valued community of concern.

> A *whole bushel of wheat is made up of single grains.*
>
> —THOMAS FULLER

Political philosopher and prominent nineteenth-century ethicist John Stuart Mill saw long ago that "whatever crushes individuality is despotism, by whatever name it may be called." No emphasis on teamwork should ever give associates reason to suspect that individual creative thought and initiative is unwelcome. That would indeed be despotism, and is as far as can be imagined from the sort of enlightened management policy now needed for leading people into the future.

I have come to believe that the tendency of Western philosophy has been to push uniqueness too far in the direction of individual autonomy and self-centeredness, and that the countervailing tendency of Eastern thought has been to push union too far in the direction of total absorption into some greater entity, as a drop of water into the ocean. What we need for proper philosophical balance and spiritual power is to keep these two needs in dynamic harmony. The union we most deeply need to experience is a form of connectedness in which we and others can make the most of our unique qualities. The uniqueness we need to embody is one that brings its distinctive strengths into the service of greater forms of union among people and, as such, is acknowledged and celebrated as a positive force within those greater unions. Our connectedness with others is the stage on which our individuality needs to play out its potential for the good of all. Likewise, our distinctiveness is the spice we bring to any community or corporate broth. There should always be a dynamic interplay between these first two spiritual needs for the proper balance to result.

> *If one of us could ascend to the heavenly realm and for a few hours accompany the divine on His daily rounds, he would see below millions of his fellow humans busily hurling themselves into the passions, sports, and action of the moment—all the while seemingly oblivious of those around him. But if our observer had the power and omniscience of the Lord, he would also feel and sense, pulsing through and vibrating from every one of us here below a desperate and unending plea, "Notice me! I want to be known, admired, and loved by the whole world!" And it is this, this glorious weakness, this dependence of us on each other, that makes some of us heroes and some of us fools—and most of us usually heroes and fools at the same time.*　　　　　　　　　　　—THE REVEREND MICHAEL BURRY

It is precisely our need to be noticed and appreciated that drives us into community and the union of joint endeavors. But it is also our need for union which spurs us to develop sufficient individual talents to qualify as contributing members of some larger, important group. Again, both needs are important, and each should be understood in relation to the other.

Unity and Diversity

Because the topic of diversity has been high on the corporate agenda in recent years, we need to make clear how unity and diversity are related, and thus what a healthy sense of union on the corporate level might involve.

Clearly, some benefits derive from living or working in an environment of homogeneity or similarity. In this context you easily feel a greater degree of immediate comfort. The more the people around you are like you, the more easily you feel that you fit in. You're confirmed in who you are and in how you think. The uneasiness of difference is not present to trouble you. You are in your element.

But there are also some strong advantages in an environment of heterogeneity or diversity. This environment will inevitably be stimulating intellectually. You are exposed to differences that you need to assimilate and understand. You're forced to think outside the normal ruts. In this context, you can develop a sense of creative openness to the new that is very exhilarating. Challenges to who you are and how you think can be the goads to personal and professional growth, bringing a great sense of fulfillment. An environment of diversity and difference is always one of learning, and learning is intimately connected with a sense of happiness in our lives.

> *Men are born equal but they are also born different.* —ERICH FROMM

Now, in any corporate endeavor, it can easily be seen that there are similarities important to have among the people involved, and that there are likewise diversities important to have. By contrast, of course, there are similarities clearly not to be sought in a workforce, or team, because they are completely irrelevant to the goal of doing good work. In most normal business contexts, it would make absolutely no sense, for example, to try to hire only people with the name Joe, or people with red hair, or right-handed people, or folks born in April. These similarities would not enhance the work environment or accelerate the pace of positive change. They would be simply bizarre. But there are similarities that are helpful if people are to work together productively. For example, everyone on a team or in a company should share some basic values. And they should possess a capacity to agree on the basic purposes and goals that will guide them.

In the same way, there are diversities it would be ridiculous to pursue and embrace. For instance, can you imagine someone sincerely saying, "We've got a lot of truth tellers around here, honest people everywhere in the company. Maybe we could use a little more diversity. . . . Let's hire some liars!"? This would be a dangerous, self-defeating form of diversity. Likewise, you don't need to recruit rude people to balance out the polite ones you've had for years, although if you find yourself in the converse situation, some countervailing action is indeed clearly appropriate. In a slightly different vein, it wouldn't make much sense to say, "Well, we've got only blondes and brunettes in this radio station, so we clearly need some redheads to attain the highest levels of competitive excellence."

However, there are diversities that are important from a purely business perspective. The people in your office should bring to their work different life experiences and experiential tacks, different ways of experiencing events on the cognitive, emotional, and attitudinal levels.

> As many men, so many minds; every one his own way.   —TERENCE

The people on your team ideally should have access to and be able to operate out of importantly different interpretive frameworks. The same facts can be taken many different ways, and any business needs people who can complement each other in their experience and inferential abilities. It can also be useful to have people on staff with diverse existential proclivities, different ways of approaching life as a whole. Again, they can augment one another's abilities and judgments best when they benefit from the broadest possible array of positive backgrounds. That way, it is less likely that anyone will be blindsided by something that no one could see coming.

> A single arrow is easily broken, but not ten in a bundle.
> —JAPANESE PROVERB

A certain strength can often be found in numbers alone. An old piece of Ethiopian folk wisdom tells us, "When spiderwebs unite, they can tie up a lion." And in The Iliad, Homer went so far as to say, "Not vain the weakest, if their force unite." So it's no surprise that human beings need and move toward union with others in both life and work. But strength in numbers is not quite the absolute it's often presented as. We often need more than numbers alone will provide. And for meeting most business challenges, I'd prefer to have a small but diverse and creative team than a big horde of same-thinkers any day. Differences in gender, race, geographic origination, ethnicity, general background, and previous employment can all be important if we are to have a creative and powerful workforce. While a blanket pursuit of diversity in itself is no more a guarantee of success than is a general insistence on similarity, a strong unity in corporate life and an empowered organization is always the result of bringing together the right similarities with the right diversities.

True Virtue and Proper Unity

The ancient Greek poet Ovid spoke of "a spirit superior to every weapon." What can create such a spirit? The great Puritan theologian and philosopher Jonathan Edwards began his 1755 essay "The Nature of True Virtue" with this definition:

> True virtue most essentially consists in *benevolence to being in general*. Or perhaps to speak more accurately, it is that consent, propensity and union of heart to being in general, which is immediately exercised in a general good will.

He then goes on to admit a page later, "When I say true virtue consists in love to being in general, I shall not be likely to be understood . . . ," but of course, in that realization he joins many other philosophers throughout the centuries. He goes on to explain,

> But my meaning is, that no affections towards particular persons or beings are of the nature of true virtue, but such as arise from a generally benevolent temper, or from that habit or frame of mind, wherein consists a disposition to love being in general.

You'll recall that we've spoken about an individual human virtue as a character strength. Virtue itself is something like an overall human strength or excellence that facilitates the attainment of proper human purposes and is tied in most intimately to the meaning of human life. Edwards sees true virtue as involving a union of the heart with "being in general," the broadest possible sort of inclusive connectedness between an individual person and surrounding reality. He suggests that no union with any other person or group of people is appropriate or virtuous that cuts us off from a greater, more general form of spiritual union. Entered into correctly, however, unity between two or more people can be the foundation for greater and more comprehensive forms of unity that reach out into the larger surrounding world.

> *Behold how good and pleasant it is for brothers to stand together in unity.* —PSALM 133:1

A love relationship is not virtuous or strengthening if it cuts us off from our other good friends. A loyalty to the department or to the team is not virtuous or truly strengthening if it is exclusive and adversarial with respect to other people in the larger organization. Every form of human union should in some sense be upwardly or outwardly open to other forms of union as well. A marriage is the basis for a family, and a family union can and should be an important building block in a community. Communities make up cities, cities belong in the larger union of states, and states make up nations. Individuals at work form teams. Many teams may be found in the same department or division, and teams can cross departmental and functional lines. Our sense of union among ourselves in our company must not preclude, but should be the foundation for, a broader union yet, with all our customers and suppliers as well as with our surrounding communities. We must not forget that the sense of solidarity or union within an organization must never conflict with, but should always support, a broader sense of civic connectedness and concern. This is how community is built, one level of commitment after another.

We've all seen how a small group of people can seek to increase its power at the expense of others with whom they're supposed to be working. This always sows the seeds of trouble within any business. And we've seen how different departments within the same organization can resist each other out of resentment, misplaced rivalry, or even just a failure to understand. Cliques can hurt the morale of any workplace. It's all this that Jonathan Edwards is writing about, even in his own time. An allegiance to "being in general" should be the ultimate context and constraint on any lesser allegiance we enter into.

Shared Values and Motivation

> *There are two forces that unite men, fear and interest.*
>
> —NAPOLÉON BONAPARTE

At the beginning of the sixteenth century, the Italian thinker Niccolò Machiavelli stated that there are two possible ways to motivate people, through love or through fear. Love, he said, is too fickle. Therefore, he reasoned, we should motivate through fear. He wrote,

> Men worry less about doing an injury to one who makes himself loved than to one who makes himself feared. The bond of love is one which men, wretched creatures that they are, break when it is to their advantage to do so; but fear is strengthened by a dread of punishment which is very effective.

For a man who was not very successful in his own lifetime, it is truly amazing how influential Machiavelli and his attitudes have become in the modern world. His words have reverberated through the centuries and seem to have far too much influence in the corporate culture of modern America.

People can indeed be motivated by fear. They can team up and work harder together because of this force. In times of war and natural disaster this is most evident. Even in tough economic times, a fear of loss and uncertainty can sometimes move people to draw more deeply on their energies to work together harder and longer.

Fear certainly seems to be a tactic often employed in the modern workplace: Keep people in fear of losing their jobs, and you keep them motivated to perform. But fear is an acid that will eat away corporate spirit as fast as anything on earth. And I believe that artificially constructed fear, the policy of scaring people by issuing threats, misrepresenting the market, and manipulating emotions, in addition to being just plain wrong, is also inevitably nothing more than a short-term motivator that always creates more problems than it solves.

I believe that Machiavelli presented us with false alternatives when he wrote of love and fear. The fear he focuses on is fear of a person, of an autocratic military leader or "prince." And correspondingly, the love he has in mind is the good feeling toward or affection for a person as well. He sees this kind of love as fickle and as too often subject to the whims of perceived self-interest. But there is another form of love that is motivationally deeper than what Machiavelli refers to here. It's close to what Napoleon had in mind when he identified the forces that unite human beings as fear and interest.

> *Joint undertakings stand a better chance when they benefit both sides.*
> —EURIPIDES

What you most deeply love, what you most fundamentally value, is at the foundation of your motivational structure. It has a grip on your thoughts, beliefs, emotions, and attitudes, as well as, through them, on your actions. You will always be most motivated to accomplish goals that you perceive as benefiting you with respect to your deepest and most important interests, your fundamental loves and values. The fickleness of human love in the sense of affection felt toward another person is often precisely a response to an altered judgment on your part concerning the relation of that person to what you most fundamentally love or value.

The most powerful motivator of people in any workplace is their sense, continually reinforced by the messages they receive and the treatment they encounter, that working well together will secure and further those things they most deeply love and value, such things as security for their families, prosperity for their communities, a sense of positive self-esteem, and an experience of meaning and pride in how they spend their days. If we love what we do, we are more likely to do it well. It's not the affection or regard for a particular person that is paramount here, but rather a deeper sense that by doing our work we are caring for our deepest, most fundamental loves.

Executives don't have to go around expounding philosophical values all the time. But I believe that it is in fact important for a business to create a values statement and a mission statement as a mirror in which employees can see their own most important convictions reflected. And I'm convinced that corporate strategic planners and goal setters ought to talk more about the basic values that lie behind specific plans and goals. But what is just as important is that everyone in the business should seek to act in such a way as to embody those deep values and show real human care and concern for all coworkers.

> *What we must decide is perhaps how we are valuable rather than how valuable we are.* —EDGAR Z. FRIEDENBERG

That's why executive parking spaces and off-limits executive dining rooms are generally such a bad idea. They egregiously exclude people and destroy any sense of a greater union throughout a company.

A sense of spiritual union in our workplaces will never make its way onto a balance sheet or into a quarterly report. It is one of those realities difficult to quantify and measure, and yet it is easy for any observant person to feel its presence or sense its absence. It draws people to work in the morning and keeps them going throughout the day. It's a foundation for sustainable excellence in changing and turbulent times. And this has always been true. If we don't pull together, we'll surely pull apart. The most perceptive of thinkers have seen this. And the best leaders have put it into practice, building unity by consistently caring for their employees and making them feel included in a shared adventure of great value.

By respecting and nurturing the twin needs for a sense of uniqueness and a feeling of union among those around us, we help ourselves as well as our associates to attain that form of corporate spirit that is the wellspring of happiness, fulfillment, and quality of the highest order in everything that we do. And nothing is more important than this.

What used to be called the "soft issues" of business will increasingly be the differentiators of sustainable excellence in every industry in the world, as we move into a new century. Ultimately—after the technology is in place, our organizations are well structured, and all processes are flowing smoothly— what will make or break any business will be the spirit of the people who do the work.

12

Usefulness and Understanding

We all have a deep spiritual need to feel useful to others, and an equally significant need to understand where we are, where we're going, and why. We all need a big-picture perspective that makes sense of our lives, something like a mental map of our experience within which we can feel that we are making a positive difference in this world.

Both these needs draw us in the direction of the general spiritual target of unity, or connectedness. A feeling of usefulness is one source for a practical experience of unity with others. A sense of positive understanding can be both an intellectual and an existential form of unity experienced along the spiritual dimension. Powerful corporate spirit depends on people feeling that both these needs are being met in their work. And strong business relations of any kind are enhanced by them as well. People need to feel useful. And people need to understand what's going on around them.

The Need for Usefulness

The ancient Greek philosophers thought of us all as teleological beings (from the Greek *telos*, "purpose"), purposive creatures who need specific goals as well as an overall mission in life. Deep down, we all need to feel as if we're making a contribution. We all want to feel we're making a positive difference in every relationship we're involved in, and in every situation where our energies and intellects are called upon. Without a feeling of usefulness, we cannot attain even a small measure of ongoing happiness in our lives. This is one reason why unemployment is never just an economic fact; it's always a much deeper spiritual problem.

> *A useless life is an early death.*   —JOHANN WOLFGANG VON GOETHE

When we cease to feel useful, we cease to feel valuable. We no longer feel alive. This is why retirement can literally kill if it is not handled properly.

A vibrant man in his seventies told me that he and three of his friends had retired the same year. He found interesting new involvements right away that drew on his talents and experience, volunteer activities that gave him a continued sense of usefulness in the world. His friends did not. After long careers of hard work, they planned in their retirements only to rest. "May they rest in peace," he said. Within two years, all three had died. The fact is that a teleological being needs to be engaged in the business of life, and to feel useful.

When my son was about seven years old, my wife and I decided one day to give him some regular jobs around the house. But when I told him about the plan, he quickly said, "Dad, I'm a kid. My job is to have fun." And I bought it. I thought to myself, OK, I guess responsibility does come early enough as it is, so maybe he should just play and have fun while he can. But after a few more weeks, I came to suspect that he was not feeling the level of fulfillment in family affairs that he was capable of. He certainly felt he was benefiting from family life, but he may not have felt he was contributing to it. And, ironically, benefits never confer the level of satisfaction that contributions do. When we finally did assign him more ongoing responsibilities, he seemed to experience a new sense of family solidarity.

This is the spiritual need most immediately behind the importance of empowerment in the workplace. When we empower people to act, to create, and to make a real difference that they themselves can perceive as valuable, we position them for an experience of deep fulfillment and meaning in what they do. We help them meet their spiritual need for uniqueness. And we assist in meeting their other fundamental spiritual need for a sense of union as well. A sense of usefulness is after all just a sense that you are making your own unique contribution to a greater union of people within which you have a valuable place. These three fundamental spiritual needs are deeply inter-connected and, properly met, are mutually reinforcing. When any one of them is not being attended to, serious consequences for the others result.

> *To crush, to annihilate a man utterly, to inflict on him the most ter-rible of punishments so that the most ferocious murderer would shudder at it and dread it beforehand, one need only give him work of an absolutely, completely useless and irrational character.*
>
> —FYODOR DOSTOYEVSKY

Having no work at all is a terrible problem. Longtime unemployment sets people adrift. And those rare individuals who discover that they have no real work to do within the confines of a paying job find themselves in nearly as bad a shape. I've talked to government employees who were going nuts because they said they had nothing to do all day. One of my parents' good friends used to complain bitterly that he showed up for work every morning at his federal agency with a novel to read because, otherwise, he would just sit and stare at his desk all day. He said he felt he couldn't quit because of the security and retirement benefits, but he was counting the days to retire-ment when he would be able to leave and get a real job. His deep spiritual need was for fruitful work, for the genuine employment of his talents and energies.

> *Employment is nature's physician and is essential to human happi-ness.*
>
> —GALEN

The Importance of Meaningful, Noble Work

Of course, having no work at all to do is not often a problem for people employed in the private sector. Or, rather, it's not usually a problem for very long. No work eventually means no job. But in some corporate contexts, having work that seems to make little or no sense may be an even worse problem, as Dostoyevsky appreciated. And this problem arises in different ways. First, some people are severely underemployed in their jobs. They are given routine, repetitive work with no opportunity for creative thought and no chance for direct personal input into changing their overall work processes for the better. A great many quality programs have sought in recent years to identify and redesign such situations. The point has been made over and over that, in order to be and stay competitive, we need the brains in addition to the bodies of everyone at work. A point less often appreciated is that we need their hearts as well.

No one at this point in history should be a corporate Sisyphus, spending all his days metaphorically pushing a rock uphill only to see it roll down once more, to be pushed back up again to no avail, and so on, ad infinitum. Human beings are creative by nature, and are goal seekers and problem solvers. Every human being needs to be an originator of ideas and a creator of structures. None of us can stand to live like a robot. Each of us needs challenges that make sense to us, challenges that get us somewhere and make us feel that we have given something of ourselves to a process that we believe in and find meaningful.

> *We do not go to work only to earn an income, but to find meaning in our lives. What we do is a large part of what we are.* —ALAN RYAN

Too many people in our companies do not see the big picture of what they do day-to-day. They do not have the opportunity really to perceive the potential magnitude of their contributions for the greater good of others. I hate to hear anyone describe their job by saying something like "I'm just a truck driver," "I'm just a secretary," "I'm just a salesman," or "I'm just a housewife." I love to hear a remark like "I drive for APA Trucking. We keep America in business," or "I'm a salesman. I put people together with products that improve their lives," or "I'm raising three wonderful children, or, to put it more accurately, two youngsters and a growing husband." There is no job productive of any good, whether product or service, that does not merit a noble description. Too many of us walk around with trivial, reductive, demeaning descriptions of what we do in the backs of our minds, haunting us and denying us the deep satisfaction that we deserve in our jobs.

We ought to all be working hard to see to it that we ourselves and the people that we work around carry in our heads and in our hearts the noblest possible images and conceptions of what we do at work. Strategic planning and goal setting at work should engage the imagination every bit as much as the mind. We should always position new initiatives in the context of the big picture for what we are doing at work, pointing out the worthwhile values that lie behind what we are striving toward and hoping to accomplish. This will give people ample opportunity to feel a deep sense of usefulness in their efforts, understanding their work to be for the sake of something valuable, however hard it might be. Most people do not mind working hard if they feel that what they are doing is noble and well worth their efforts.

> *Far and away the best prize that life offers is the chance to work hard at work worth doing.* —THEODORE ROOSEVELT

How can we help people to see the big picture? The most obvious but probably best answer is to talk about it more. Top executives and management people should regularly sketch it out and reinforce it in meetings, in newsletters, and through any other creative means available. They should tell stories that illustrate the nobility of what everyone in the organization is doing together. Another way recently being tried is to encourage all employees in our organizations to talk with associates who work outside their offices or functional structures. Everyone thereby comes to have a greater appreciation of the whole within which they are an important part.

Skill Building and the Big Picture

Yet another way of giving people a better big picture of what they are doing has increasingly been explored in recent years, and it is a strategy that, if implemented carefully, can indeed enhance employees' sense of usefulness. Many companies have lately been encouraging their people to some extent to learn each other's jobs, to diversify their skills, and to build up areas that have been in the past personal weaknesses. This can often be a good way of bringing people to understand and appreciate those facets of organizational life they previously may have taken for granted. As they learn to do more of the jobs vital to the business, they come to appreciate the value of their own work within its overall context. And they become more useful to an organization that may be called upon to do more and more with less and less. Multiskilled people can obviously serve in a greater variety of roles.

After many decades of increasing specialization in organizational life, a bit more generalism can be healthy in many ways. But only as long as it's not overdone. Recently, while I was visiting with a large service company, I heard a number of highly accomplished frontline associates complain that they were being overly pressured to develop new skills and strengthen areas of weakness rather than building on their true strengths and talents. They felt that they were being taken away from those areas where they could best serve both the company and their clients. They worried that they were being molded into interchangeable parts in such a way that they would no longer be able to perform at their unique levels of personal excellence. They were in danger of feeling less rather than more useful.

> Let each man pass his days in that wherein his skill is greatest.
>
> —SEXTUS PROPERTIUS

That's why multitasking and diversification of skill building should not be overdone. We all have unique clusters of talents and experiences that are not universally replicable. We each have distinctive strengths and should be encouraged to put our best talents to work in what we do. To a point, the more we can do, the more useful we can feel. But we should never be made to feel that we are just interchangeable resources.

> Nothing is more important than creating an environment in which people feel they make a difference. You can't feel good about what you're doing unless you think you're making a difference.
>
> —JACK STACK

The Depth of the Need

The most surprising account I have ever heard of the spiritual need for usefulness being met comes out of the Texas State Penitentiary at Huntsville, where the inmates on death row have been allowed to leave their cells and go to work making uniforms for the prison guards. Now, at first blush, you might think that this is cruel to the point of being slightly sadistic—prisoners are put to work clothing the people who are going to kill them. You might think that this would surely exterminate any shred of positive human feeling that otherwise manages to exist in such circumstances. But journalists who have visited Huntsville have reported a noticeable increase in morale among the prisoners doing the work. Even prisoners need to feel as if they're contributing, no matter how extreme the circumstances. Everyone has a deep spiritual need to feel useful.

The same force that can bring death-row prisoners positive morale can certainly build positive corporate spirit in our businesses. We need to help the people around us feel as if they are making a difference. We need to be sure that everyone at work is feeling useful. David Packard, cofounder of Hewlett Packard, has reported that it was a spiritual calling "to do something useful" that led him to build that great company. The need for a sense of usefulness is a great force in human life, a spiritual need that will not be denied.

The Need for Understanding

I can't believe how many people have said to me that when they stop to think about their lives, they feel as if they're lost in the woods without a map or a compass. Of course, a sense of being lost in life is not a distinctively modern phenomenon. The poet Dante began his *Inferno* with the lines

> Halfway through the journey of our life,
> Having strayed from the right path and lost it,
> I awoke to find myself in a dark wood.

Where are we? Where are we going? And why? We all need to have some sense of our bearings in this world. We need a map for our lives, as well as some strong sense of direction. Too many of us suffer because of basic misunderstandings about life, deep misunderstandings that we often do not see as such until we are "halfway through the journey of our life." But the sooner we begin to find our proper path, the better. We all have a deep spiritual need to understand our work and our place in the world. Understanding is a fundamental condition for satisfaction and deep fulfillment in what we do as well as for who we are.

> *I can only say this to you, that he who does not know who he is, and for what purpose he exists, and what is this world, and with whom he is associated, and what things are the good and the bad, and the beautiful and the ugly, and who neither understands discourse nor demonstration, nor what is true nor what is false, and who is not able to distinguish them, will neither desire according to nature nor turn away nor move upward, nor intentionally act, nor assent, nor dissent nor suspend his judgment: to say all in a few words, he will go about dumb and blind, thinking that he is somebody, but being nobody.*
> —EPICTETUS

Let's begin by looking at the importance of understanding for human happiness on a very general level. I believe there are at large in our culture right now a number of conceptual misunderstandings that are responsible for a great deal of the unhappiness and dissatisfaction of our time. This is manifested in a malaise that is felt both in people's personal lives and in their professional careers. We are in danger of losing sight of some of the most ancient goods for human life, whose role is being usurped by some modern impostors or counterfeits that purport to be identical with those true goods but that are poor imitations. Let me give a few examples of what I mean.

ANCIENT GOOD	MODERN COUNTERFEIT
Wisdom	Cleverness
Dignity	Glamour
Truth	Expediency
Beauty	Titillation
Goodness	Pleasantness
Character	Personality
Reputation	Fame
Respect	Fear

For example, the ancient good of wisdom is in danger of being eclipsed by the modern substitute of cleverness. When I was a graduate student at

Yale, I was surprised to find that hardly anyone I met seemed to be pursuing wisdom. Nearly everyone appeared instead to be intent on cultivating cleverness. We were all more likely to become show-offs than sages.

> *Confucius say cleverness is not wisdom.*
> —FORTUNE COOKIE PROCLAMATION

I recall vividly my first semester at that venerable institution. Conversational fireworks were always flying. People were dropping names like hot potatoes and quoting from memory authors I had never even read. By the end of the first week on campus, I remember wondering how I ever got admitted into graduate school at all, convinced that everyone else at Yale was vastly smarter and better educated than me. What I didn't realize until about six weeks later was that all the first-year graduate students were thinking exactly the same thing. Not about me, I hasten to add, but about themselves, as judged against everyone else, including, to my utter astonishment, me. We all often pretended to understand what we really didn't grasp, fearing to be thought less clever than our peers, who were also for the most part just pretending to know what they actually knew little of at all. We thereby deprived ourselves of much of the education that could have been ours for the taking.

> *Nothing doth more hurt in a state than that cunning men pass for wise.*
> —FRANCIS BACON

Too many people nowadays confuse glamour with dignity. I've had people who work in factories practically apologize to me about their jobs. Because their jobs weren't glamorous, they seemed to assume that they were somehow not dignified. And I've had some people who own factories recount to me almost apologetically what they do as well, because in their own minds, as well as in the apparently general estimation of the culture, the product that they make is "a little boring," not glamorous, and thus, they seemed to be conveying, not quite dignified.

But glamour is not the same thing as dignity. And any society that fails to realize that is in trouble. In fact, any culture that loses sight of the intrinsic dignity of hard work and skilled labor is a culture in deep trouble indeed.

A good woodworker or a master mechanic should have every bit as much dignity as a professor, or a CEO, a surgeon, or a senator.

In all my years of teaching at Notre Dame, I never saw myself as preparing my students to live the lifestyles of the rich and famous. I wanted instead to prepare them to live the lifestyles of the wise and happy. A life need not be glamorous to be honorable and dignified and full of meaning.

Now, don't get me wrong. I'm not saying that there is anything inherently wrong with either cleverness or glamour. They can be wonderful spices to life—as long as they are not substitutes for wisdom and dignity. A failure to understand the difference is responsible for a lot of people chasing the wrong things in their lives. Likewise, the ancient good of truth is in danger in many circles of yielding to the modern counterfeit of expediency. People cease to ask, "Is it true?" and concern themselves only with the question, "Will it work?" Of course, there is nothing at all wrong with being pragmatic, as long as a concern with expediency is not allowed to eclipse our grasp of what is true and real.

We should realize that beauty is not the same thing as titillation. Goodness is not the same thing as pleasantness. When hiring, it's not enough to ask, "Is he easy to get along with?" or "Does she have a pleasant personality?" We must also always ask "Is this a good person?"—a distinct, though related, question. Character is not the same thing as personality.

The ancient good of reputation, as well, is in danger of being replaced by the modern hankering after fame, or celebrity, at almost any cost. In our times a man or woman is known by what he or she does. If we want to be well thought of, we should do well. But public opinion should always be secondary to our focus on the quality of what we contribute.

> He preferred to be, rather than to seem, good; hence the less he sought fame, the more it pursued him.   —SALLUST, REFERRING TO CATO

Many of these modern conceptual confusions are based on a failure to distinguish appearances from realities. But whatever the cause, they have common effects. Accepting counterfeits and losing sight of the ancient goods blocks that kind of fundamental understanding of life that is a necessary condition for any mature, adult happiness of an enduring kind. If we don't understand the differences between such different things, we cannot steer our way through life successfully.

Edmund Burke once remarked, about the real strengths of human life, "There are few of those virtues which are not capable of being imitated, and even outdone in many of their most striking effects, by the worst of vices." But imitation cannot last. We need to grasp firmly the difference between virtue and vice, between good and the mere appearance of good, between spice and substance, if we want to give proper direction to our thoughts and efforts. In any corporate endeavor, we must see to it as much as possible that everyone involved understands the differences between such things. Otherwise, goals will be pursued and things done that will not have lasting consequences for good.

> The supreme end of education is expert discernment in all things— the power to tell the good from the bad, the genuine from the counterfeit, and to prefer the good and the genuine to the bad and the counterfeit.
>
> —SAMUEL JOHNSON

Contextual Understanding

One well-known company president who employs a total of about four hundred people likes to say that he has a sales force of four hundred. He believes that everyone who works for him is capable of selling the company's products, because they all know the business well enough and believe in it from the heart. He is convinced that what separates an ordinary employee from an entrepreneur is just knowledge, excitement, a sense of mission, and a reward system that makes everybody feel like an owner. A sense of understanding can be highly motivating. The more people know, and the more they understand, the more they can do for the common enterprise.

But some executives worry about sharing too much knowledge of the business. They point to companies like the old IBM, which prided itself on teaching its people all about its products and as a result ended up with many of those people out in the world years later working as extremely knowledgeable competitors.

The example here is instructive. IBM always had a strong corporate culture, but some would say that it was, in the old IBM, a stifling one. I believe that in a nurturing company environment, people will not be so likely to leave and become competitors. They will instead more likely be inspired to become internal entrepreneurs. Is there then no risk at all? Of course there is, but risk is often related to reward, and a proper environment makes this a risk worth taking. Successful companies like 3M have been demonstrating this for a long time. Without an extensive sharing of product, process, and market understanding, the pinnacle of corporate excellence is just not available.

> *Hire and promote first on the basis of integrity; second, motivation; third; capacity; fourth, understanding; fifth, knowledge; and last and least, experience. Without integrity, motivation is dangerous; without motivation, capacity is impotent; without capacity, understanding is limited; without understanding, knowledge is meaningless; without knowledge, experience is blind. Experience is easy to provide and quickly put to use by people with all the other qualities.*
>
> —DEE HOCK

Provided and used properly, more understanding is reliably preferable to less understanding. In one sense, we've come full circle back to the importance of the intellectual dimension of human experience and the power of truth in organizational enterprises. But the kind of understanding that is distinctively a part of the spiritual dimension goes beyond the merely intellectual. It is never just a matter of the head, but is also a state of the heart. It is an existential sense of the whats, the hows, and the whys of your work. It is something we pick up, and pass along to others as much by what we do as by what we say, and by the way we do it.

An openness of spirit, an enthusiasm, the collaborative process itself, can communicate a sense of understanding to all participants, within the bounds of any joint effort, within the workday existence of any organization. When people feel that sort of understanding on an emotional level as well as in their heads, you have fertile soil for powerful corporate spirit, a context within which people can flourish as human beings, with talents, experiences, and contributions to make to the world. Linked with all the other spiritual needs, a respect for and nurturing of this need can move an organization in the direction of its own greatest and most sustainable forms of excellence.

EPILOGUE

Creating Corporate Excellence

I have walked this earth for thirty years and, out of gratitude, want to leave some souvenir. —VINCENT VAN GOGH

Corporate excellence is a form of human excellence. It is produced by people who believe in what they are doing. It is sustained by people who are supported in what they're doing by a culture that respects and nurtures all four fundamental dimensions of their genuinely human experience: the intellectual dimension, the aesthetic dimension, the moral dimension, and the spiritual dimension. Organizational success and inner personal satisfaction require significant doses of truth, beauty, goodness, and unity. These four timeless values are the four foundations of sustainable excellence and human flourishing. Nothing less will do.

We have a tendency not to sink our roots deeply enough. We look around us at the best practices of other organizations that seem to work, and we try to emulate them in our own endeavors. We don't often analyze exactly why they work, or investigate what it is in human nature that makes them work. And so we're surprised when they fail to transfer to our companies as well as we had expected. We fret that maybe we haven't been motivated enough, or that we've made some technical mistake. We send out memos and tweak processes. We read one more management book. We seek insight. But we don't dig deeply enough. We don't often enough seek genuine wisdom.

We need to thrust our roots down as far as possible into the innermost springs of human thought and behavior. We need to find the most universal and reliable touchstones of sustainable excellence and the most fundamental keys to ultimate motivation. In the end, it is only the rock-bottom truth about human happiness and fulfillment that will give us enduring foundations for our work together.

People will not face the challenges of change and risk happily unless they feel supported as human beings. We cannot be at our creative and energetic best unless we are planted in rich, fertile soil. Wisdom about the sources of human happiness and human motivation must be the lifeblood of any organization. The greatest insights of the wisest people who have ever lived should be our guide in these challenging and exciting times.

Truth, beauty, goodness, and unity: These four foundations should be the ultimate supports of organizational life, and for that matter, of all positive human relationships. They should govern what we do together as families, as communities, and as businesses. How exactly do they apply to your particular circumstances right now? As Socrates once admitted about himself, being a philosopher doesn't mean that I have all the answers. It only means that I can help you ask all the right questions. If you ask yourself how you can enhance the level of truth, the experience of beauty, the assurance of goodness, and the sense of unity felt by the people who work around you and with you, you will be asking the right questions for creating positive and powerful corporate spirit.

The process of creating a new corporate spirit and refurbishing these foundations for business excellence will not be simple or quick. But it is worth all the thought and effort you can put into it. And it can never take place effectively unless all of us attempting to make a difference in our organizations are guided by two beacons, a nearly magical pair of powerful qualities rarely found balanced together in human life. I discovered their intertwined importance in an unusual way, and I want to share it with you.

The True Spirit of Greatness

A few years ago, I got to know the prominent television producer Norman Lear. I have benefited from many of his insights about life, but one day I received a letter from him that topped it all. He explained that he had recently been on a panel discussion to talk about religion and public policy in America. He recounted that in answer to a question, he had struggled for some minutes to articulate his feeling that the older he got, the more he came to see "the individual's insignificance in God's great scheme of things," and yet that it was precisely this particular insight that made him feel "bigger and more important all the time." He said that he had verbally twisted and turned trying to make sense of that apparently paradoxical insight, but that he had felt he was having little success.

At the end of the session, an elderly man came up to him and introduced himself as Rabbi Fields. He said, "Mr. Lear, there is an ancient piece of Hasidic wisdom that captures well what you were attempting to say. I'll send it to you." Lear then adds in the letter, "It has meant so much to me that I want to share it with you." The quote:

> A man should always wear a garment with two pockets. In one pocket, there should be a note which reads, "I am but dust and ashes." In the other pocket, there should be a paper which says, "For me, the world was created."

Lear then closes by saying "Isn't that terrific?"

I read it and read it, over and over. I sat and pondered. "I am but dust and ashes"; "For me, the world was created." And then it hit me. This is the magical combination of human attitudes, the pair of dispositions most likely to draw the best out of the people around us: in reverse order, the inspiration of nobility and the relational demeanor of humility.

> *Nobility is the one and only virtue.* —JUVENAL

"For me, the world was created." People are inspired over the long run only by this sense of nobility in who they are and what they are doing. If you can convey a sense of nobility to the people around you, you can unlock their deepest potential. If you can tap into your own sense of nobility, you can gain from that the determination and persistence to initiate any important changes that need to be made, and you can stick with the process in good spirit through all the difficulties you may encounter along the way. A sense of nobility in what they are doing will go far toward encouraging people around you to do the right thing for positive corporate spirit. It will draw individuals on toward a wonderful shared future.

But nobility by itself is never enough. We all need a sense of humility as well. Nobility without humility can easily generate arrogance and presumptuousness. And, of course, humility without nobility is ineffective and impotent. It is the combination of the two that is so powerful.

> *We are all worms. But I do believe that I am a glow worm.*
> —WINSTON CHURCHILL

The Tao Te Ching says that the ocean is the greatest of all bodies of water because it is lower than the rest; they empty themselves into it. This is one of the most profound insights about leadership I have ever come across. The nobility of the ocean, its greatness, is portrayed here as a result of its humility, or its lowness. Too many leaders, executives, and managers plow their way through life, fired up by a sense of nobility but blinded to the importance of humility in their dealings with others.

"I am but dust and ashes." What can I alone accomplish? But remember, for me the world was created. If I can open myself to what is out there in the world beyond the boundaries of my own small self, if I can lower myself into a state of humble openness to receive what others have to offer, then they are much more likely to pour themselves out into me and help me accomplish the most difficult and the most worthy of tasks.

With these qualities, nobility and humility, each of us can position ourselves to contribute that which we are here to accomplish—creative love, the tasks of loving creation. We can create first and foremost an environment, a context, a culture, and a soil in which other human beings can flourish and make their contributions along with ours. We can contribute to human happiness, and human excellence. With both nobility and humility we can work together to reinvent corporate spirit for our time, to restore the human soul to business and make all our business endeavors the best and the most meaningful that they are capable of being.

I am firmly convinced that if we are prepared to philosophize in all the right ways about the crucial challenge of corporate spirit, and equally prepared to do something with what we learn, we can attain and sustain that level of corporate and individual excellence we all want, as well as that depth of personal satisfaction and happiness we all need. We then can make our mark in this world in the most positive way possible.

If Aristotle ran General Motors, I think this is what he would do. Why indeed should we settle for anything less?